Text copyright © 1985 by Susan E. Kalbfleisch
Illustrations copyright © 1985 by Laurie McGugan
First published in Canada by Kids Can Press, Toronto, Ontario.

Printed in the United States of America.

1 2 3 4 5 6 7 8 9 10

Library of Congress Cataloging-in-Publication Data
Kalbfleisch, Susan.
Jump! : the new jump rope book.
Previously published as: Skip to it! c1985.
Summary: An introduction to jumping rope with instructions for easy and advanced tricks.
1. Rope skipping—Juvenile literature. [1. Rope skipping]   I. McGugan, Laurie, ill.   II. Title.
GV498.K35   1987   796.2   86-23578
ISBN 0-688-06929-0
ISBN 0-688-06930-4 (pbk.)

SUSAN KALBFLEISCH

ILLUSTRATIONS BY LAURIE McGUGAN

JUMP!

THE NEW JUMP ROPE BOOK

WILLIAM MORROW & CO., INC. / NEW YORK

Contents

For everyone who enjoys skipping — but especially for Beth.

Thanks to Laurie, Trish, Andy, and the Hamilton Hoppers
Skipping Team whom I have had the pleasure of coaching.

Jumping rope is fun! It's also great exercise. And everyone — boy or girl, young or old — can do it.

It makes good athletic sense to warm up and cool down when you skip. The older you are, the more important the warm up. If you're an adult and you haven't been exercising lately, it's wise to have a check-up before you begin. Always skip at a comfortable rate, and stop if you begin to feel any discomfort.

With skipping, as with any exercise, use common sense.

Introduction

Jumping rope is hundreds of years old, and turns up in almost every country in the world. It may be only a slight exaggeration to say, "Everyone skips."

Some of the earliest skipping ropes were pieces of cord from nearby spinning mills, or "sash" cords from window pulls. A lucky child in 16th-century England might have had a rope with handles made from the bobbin spindles of a mill's weaving machines. Cow ropes were used for skipping in New Zealand; rubber thongs by children in Spain. In Hungary, kids used plaited straw; in Sweden, stiff wicker. French children skipped with string ropes woven on spool looms. Jump ropes of wild grapevines are still common among the Cherokee Indians; in Barbados, native vines are soaked in tubs to keep them soft and flexible between uses.

Ropes have been around for a long time, and so have the rhymes, games, contests, and exercises that are part of skipping. Skipping is fabulous exercise. The most basic jump requires coordination and skill, as well as rhythm, balance, and endurance. Skipping conditions the heart and lungs, and tones muscles. It can be done inside or outside. You can perform tricks with your rope and skip to the beat of popular music, alone or with friends.

Skipping tricks aren't hard to learn — they just take some time and practice.

There are several important things to remember when skipping.
• Make sure your rope is the right length (see page 11).
• Always wear running shoes when you skip.
• Begin slowly; stop if you feel any physical discomfort.
• Always warm up before you skip and cool down after.

Begin by learning the basic Two-Foot Bounce. Then work your way through the tricks in order. Master the Easy Tricks before you try the Advanced Tricks. Remember that practice is important; skipping takes time to learn.

When you have learned a few of the steps, try skipping to music.

However you skip — alone, with a partner, with music, or without — think of skipping as a creative exercise. And have fun!

Getting Ready

You can skip almost anywhere, although a smooth, flat, level surface works best. Make sure that you can turn your rope without hitting objects (such as the ceiling or your furniture) — or your friends.

Wear comfortable clothes along with running shoes and socks. Don't skip without shoes.

A skipping rope can be made of clothes line or plastic; it can have knots as handles, plastic handles, or no handles at all. You can do the tricks in this book with most cord-style skipping ropes. However, a beaded skipping rope is advised, because it will turn more easily, even if you turn it very slowly. This makes learning tricks easier.

A beaded skipping rope is constructed of plastic pieces strung over nylon cord with flexible plastic handles.

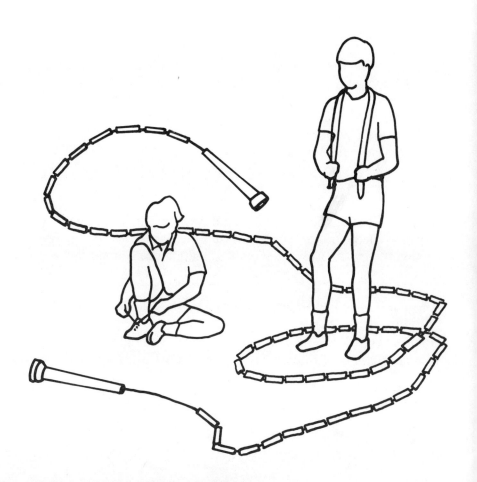

No matter what kind of rope you use, it must be the proper length.

Most skipping ropes can be adjusted. To make sure that your rope is the right length:

• Stand on the centre of the rope.
• Hold the handles (or ends of the cord if your rope has no handles) so that they reach your armpits. This is the correct length.

The boy in the picture has a skipping rope that is the right length for him.

When you're dressed properly and with a rope of the correct length — do some warm up activities for about five minutes (see pages 12-15). Now you're ready to start skipping! After you finish your skipping session, cool down by repeating the same exercises for five minutes.

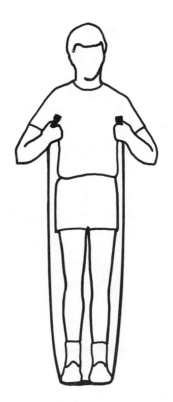

Warming Up/Cooling Down – Shoulder Shrug

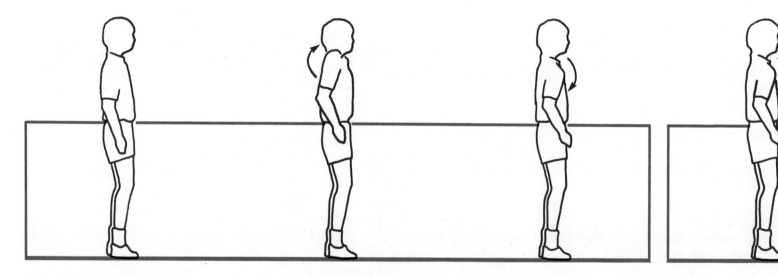

Stand up straight with your arms at your sides and your feet a little apart, knees slightly bent.

Make a small forward circle with both shoulders at the same time.

Continue to circle your shoulders forward five more times.

Circle your shoulders backwards five times too.

12

Knees Up

Don't forget to warm up for at least five minutes before you begin to skip.

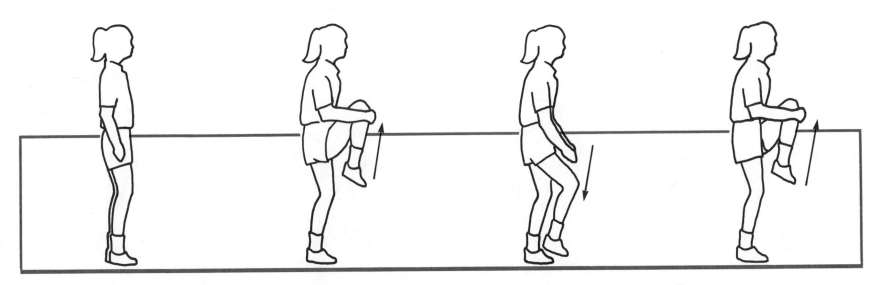

Stand up straight with your arms at your sides, your feet a little apart, and your knees slightly bent.

Keeping your body straight, raise your right knee until you can grasp your leg just below the knee with both hands. Pull your knee upward as high as you can toward your chest. If it hurts, you're pulling your knee up too high.

Slowly lower your right leg to the starting position.

Raise and lower your left knee the same way as you did your right.

Repeat the exercise five more times with each leg.

Reach for Your Toes

Always remember to stretch slowly so that muscles do not pull and hurt. And don't bounce as you bend forward — it can hurt your back!

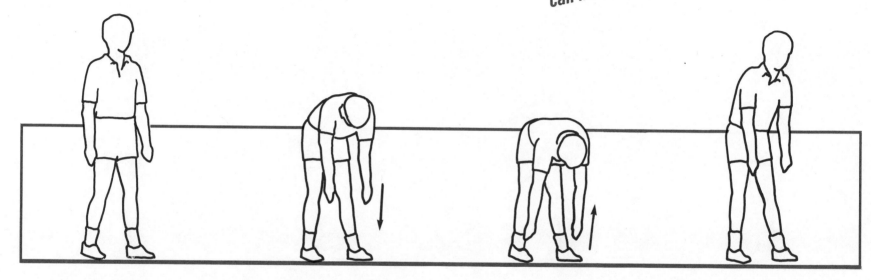

Stand up straight with your arms at your sides, feet about shoulder width apart.

Bend forward *slowly* from the waist while stretching your hands toward your toes. Keep your heels on the ground. (You don't have to touch your toes — just stretch as far as you can.)

Slowly return to the starting position.

Stretch toward your toes five more times.

Walk on the Spot

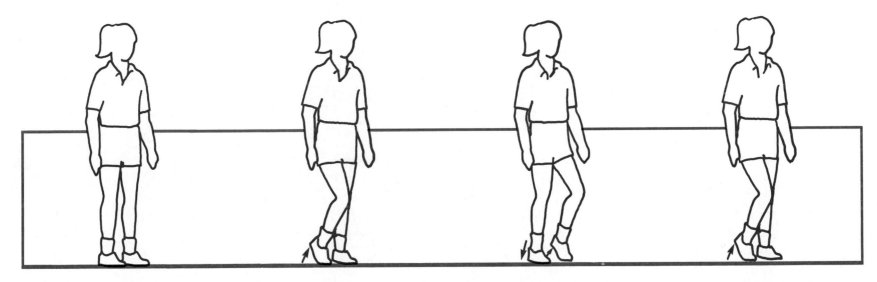

Stand up straight with your arms at your sides, feet a little apart.

Lift your right heel high off the ground while keeping your right toes on the ground. Your weight is on your left foot.

As you lower your right heel back to the ground, lift the left heel high off the ground, but keep your left toes on the ground. Your weight is on your right foot.

Continue walking on the spot by alternating your heels for one minute.

Learning to Skip
Footwork

Do not use a rope!

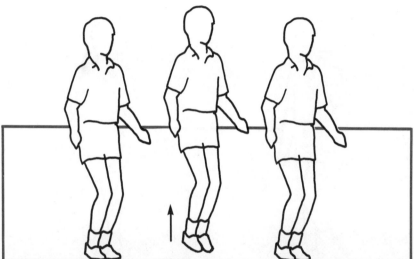

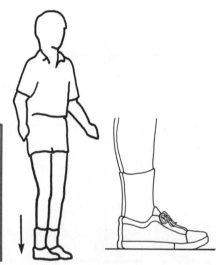

Practise bouncing (jumping) on the balls of your feet. Your heels don't usually touch the ground when you skip.

Relax and bend your knees a little on each bounce. Both feet lift from the ground and then land on the ground at the same time. Each jump should be just high enough for a rope to pass under your feet, about 2 cm (one inch) off the floor.

Once in a while, put your heels down on the ground as you land. If you don't, you could over-stretch the muscles in the backs of your legs.

Rope Turning

Stand still to practise rope turning. Don't try to jump or skip yet!

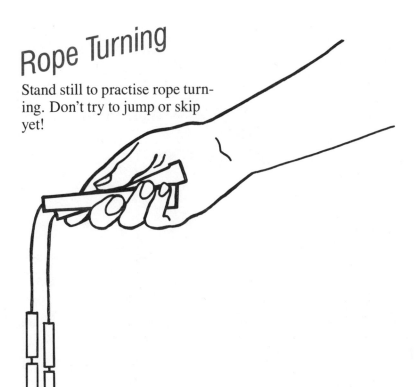

Grasp both handles in your right hand.

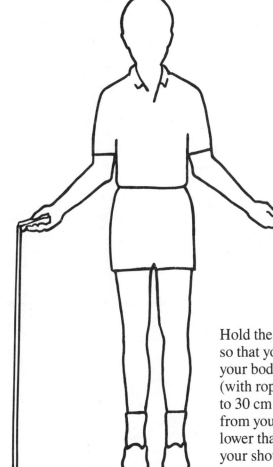

Hold the rope to your right side so that your elbow is close to your body, but your right hand (with rope handles) is about 25 to 30 cm (10 to 12 inches) away from your body, and a little lower than your waist. Relax your shoulders.

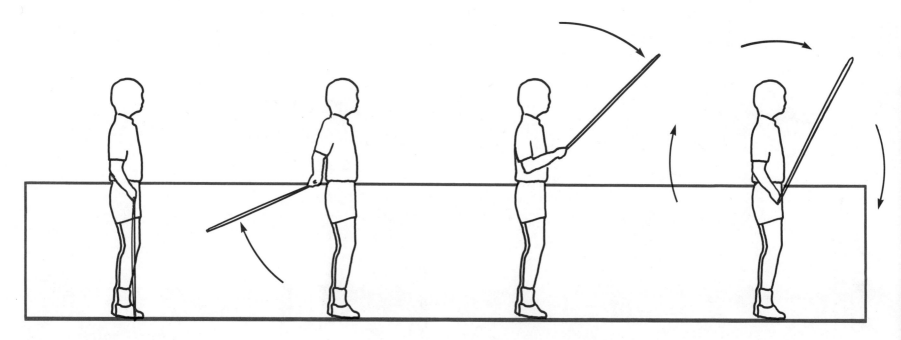

Now that the rope and your body are in the correct position, swing the rope in a circle at your right side so that it touches the ground on each turn. Your lower arm must make a full circle for the first turn to get the rope moving.

Continue to turn the rope forward using your wrist. Your arm should barely move.

Practise until the rope is turning steadily and easily, at a relaxed speed. Then switch the rope to your left hand and practise turning on your left side.

Beginning to Skip
Footwork with Rope Turning

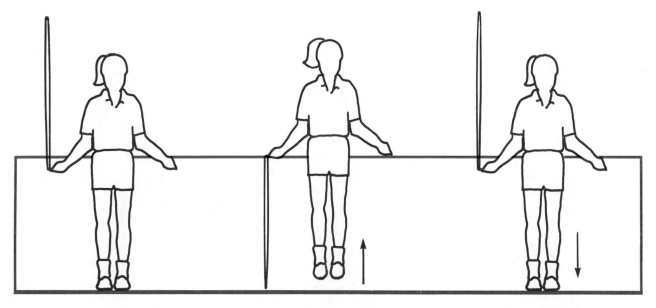

After you have practised first the footwork and then the rope turning, try to put them together. It's still not time to jump over the rope!

Grasp both handles with your right hand.

Swing your rope in a forward circle at your right side (see page 18).

Just as the rope hits the ground, jump up, both feet together, beside the rope.

Continue to turn the rope and jump each time it hits the ground. Then practise turning the rope on your left side with your left hand and jump beside the rope each time it hits the ground.

Skipping over the Rope

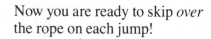

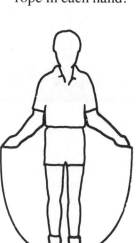

Now you are ready to skip *over* the rope on each jump!

Hold one handle (or end) of the rope in each hand.

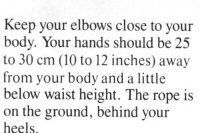

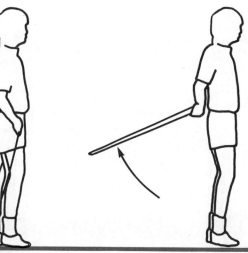

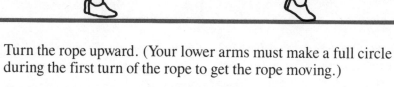

Keep your elbows close to your body. Your hands should be 25 to 30 cm (10 to 12 inches) away from your body and a little below waist height. The rope is on the ground, behind your heels.

Turn the rope upward. (Your lower arms must make a full circle during the first turn of the rope to get the rope moving.)

Continue to turn the rope so that it comes forward over your head and then down toward your feet.

Just as the rope is about to touch the ground, jump up, keeping both feet together. Continue to turn the rope forward with your

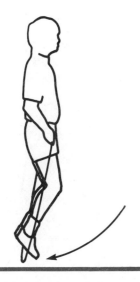

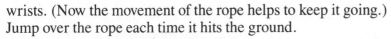

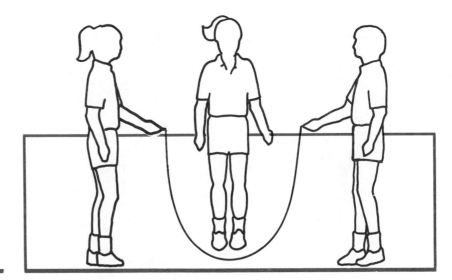

wrists. (Now the movement of the rope helps to keep it going.) Jump over the rope each time it hits the ground.

Remember that your hands move in tiny circles to turn the rope; your arms only move a little.

Jump each time that the rope goes under your feet. This is called a Two-Foot Bounce.

If you have trouble jumping over the rope while you turn it, go back and practise footwork and then practise rope turning.

If you are still having trouble after repeating the footwork and the turning, ask two friends to help you. Have each friend take an end of your rope and turn it for you. You can then concentrate on your jumping. When you feel confident and your jumping has improved, try turning the rope by yourself again.

Skipping Backwards

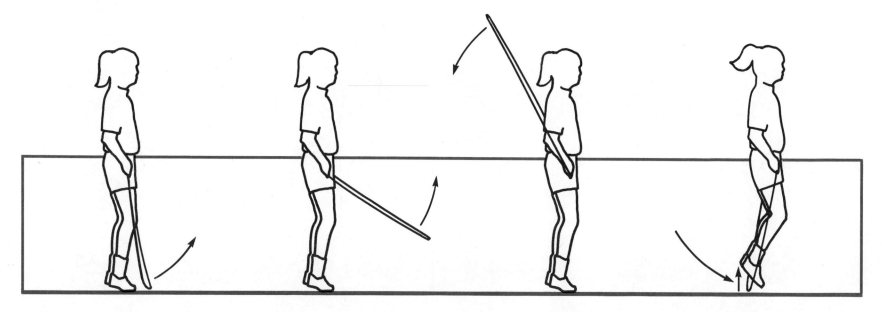

Hold the rope as you did when skipping forward, but begin with it in front of your feet.

Using small circles of your hands, turn your rope backwards. Your arms hardly move at all, except during the first turn of the rope to get it moving.

Just as the rope is about to hit the ground behind your feet, jump up, both feet together. Continue to turn the rope backwards and jump over the rope each time it hits the ground.

The Easy Tricks
Some Important Notes

Before learning any of the other tricks, make sure that you can do at least 20 Two-Foot Bounces in a row.

Each trick requires a bounce over the rope each time the rope turns.

The Easy Tricks are in order of difficulty and it is recommended that you learn them in order, from the easier to the more difficult. Master all the Easy Tricks before you try the Advanced Tricks.

Before you try a new trick with your rope, always do at least eight Two-Foot Bounces before the new step. You'll feel more comfortable with the rhythm of your skipping and the new trick will then be easier to do.

Many of the Easy Tricks instruct you to stand on a base line. You can pretend that there is a line in front of you. If you're skipping outside, there may be a line on the sidewalk you can use as your reference point. But some people have trouble visualizing an imaginary line. If you do, you can put a piece of masking tape measuring about 30 cm (12 inches) on the ground where you're skipping and that can serve as your base line.

As you become a better skipper, you may wish to try the Easy Tricks while skipping backwards, or even while you travel (move) about.

Some Reminders

Make sure your rope is the proper length.

A jump is the same thing as a bounce.

Warm up before you start to skip and cool down afterwards.

Skip on the balls of your feet. But from time to time put your heels down to the ground as you bounce, to prevent sore legs.

Skipping is great exercise, but be careful not to overdo it.

Practise each new trick without your rope until you can do it well — then try it while jumping over your rope.

Don't get upset if you get tangled in the rope — it happens to the best skippers! Just untangle yourself and keep practising.

Have fun!

Two-Foot Bounce

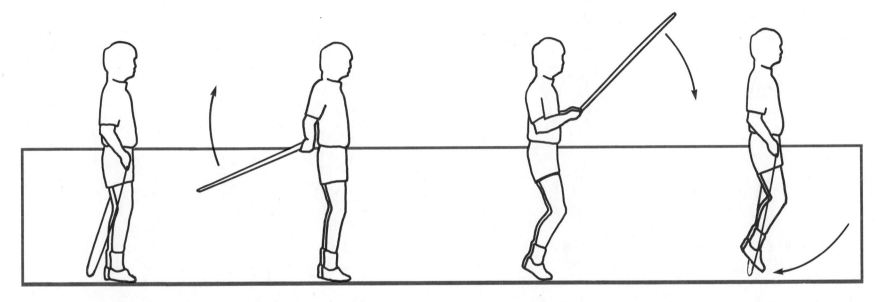

This is the basic jumping step. It is also the starting step for most skipping tricks. Begin with the rope on the ground behind your heels.

Turn the rope upward. Your lower arms must make a full circle during the first turn of the rope to get it moving.

Continue to turn the rope so that it comes from behind, up over your head, and then down toward your feet.

Just as the rope is about to touch the ground, jump up, keeping both feet together. Continue to turn your rope forward. After the first turn, your *wrists* turn the rope, not your arms. Now the movement of the rope helps to keep it going. Jump over the rope each time it hits the ground.

One-Foot Bounce

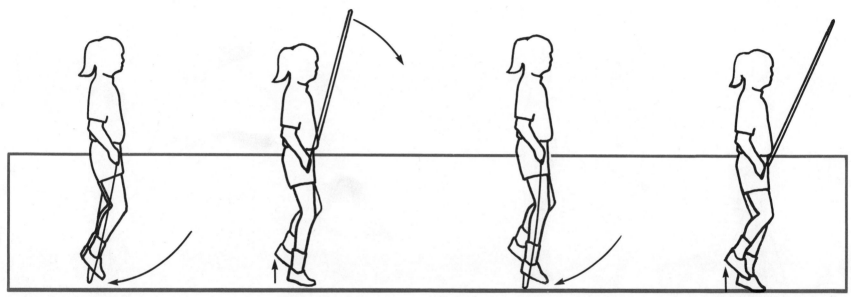

On one turn of the rope, bounce with both feet together. (This means that the rope makes one complete turn and, just as the rope hits the ground, you jump over it.)

On the next turn of the rope, bounce on your right foot. At the same time, keep your left foot a little behind and raised so that it does not touch the ground.

Continue by bouncing on your right foot. (Don't put your left foot on the ground.) Practise 8 to 16 right-foot bounces in a row.

Then practise bouncing 8 to 16 times on your left foot.

Alternating Step

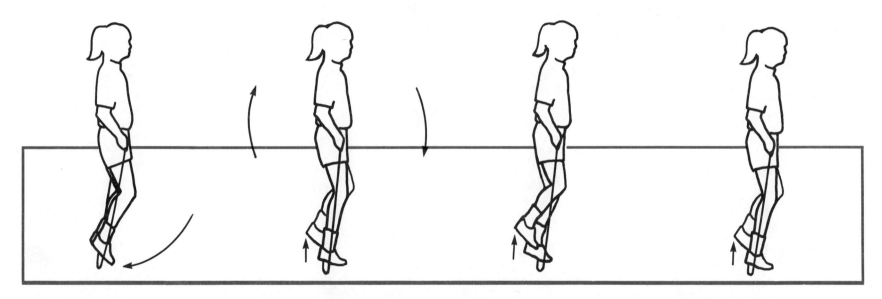

On one turn of the rope, bounce with both feet together.

On the next turn of the rope, bounce on your right foot. At the same time, keep your left foot a little behind and raised so that it does not touch the ground.

On the next turn of the rope, bounce on your left foot. At the same time, keep your right foot a little behind and raised so that it does not touch the ground.

Continue by bouncing on the right foot, then the left foot, and so on. (As you skip more quickly and turn the rope faster, this Alternating Step becomes running on the spot.)

Heel Tap

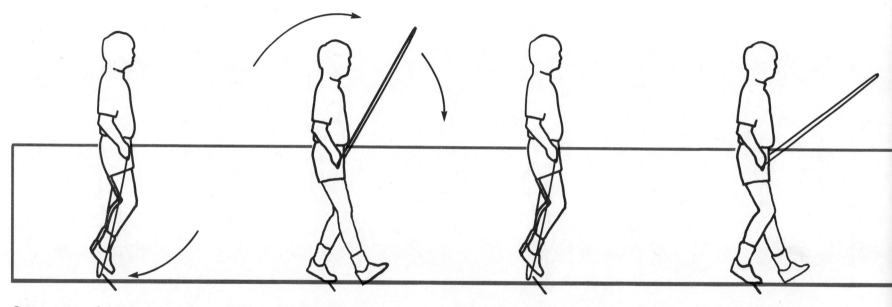

On one turn of the rope, bounce with both feet together on your base line.

On the next turn of the rope, bounce so that your left foot lands on the line. At the same time, tap your right heel lightly on the ground in front of the line.

On the next turn of the rope, bounce with both feet together on the line.

On the next turn of the rope, bounce so that your right foot lands on the line. At the same time, tap your left heel lightly on the ground in front of the line.

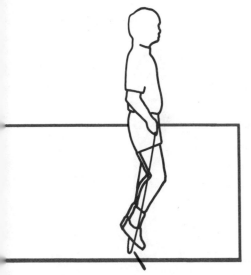

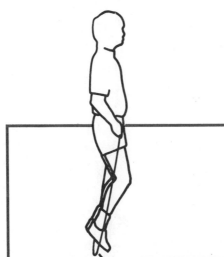

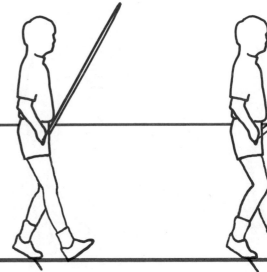

Continue by bouncing with both feet together, tapping right heel forward, bouncing both feet together, tapping left heel forward, and so on.

The Advanced Heel Tap leaves out all of the Two-Foot Bounces in the Heel Tap.

On one turn of the rope, bounce with both feet together on your base line.

On the next turn of the rope, bounce so that your left foot lands on the line. At the same time, tap your right heel lightly on the ground in front of the line.

On the next turn of the rope, bounce so that your right foot lands on the line. At the same time, tap your left heel lightly on the ground in front of the line. Continue to tap right, left, and so on.

 Toe Tap

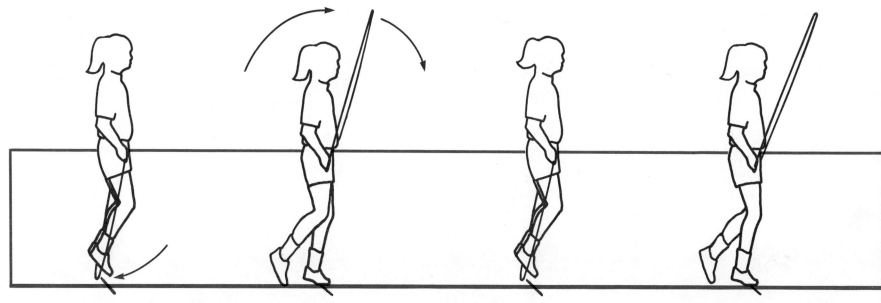

On one turn of the rope, bounce with both feet together on your base line.

On the next turn of the rope, bounce so that your left foot lands on the line. At the same time, tap your right toe lightly on the ground behind the line.

On the next turn of the rope, bounce with both feet together on the line.

On the next turn of the rope, bounce so that your right foot lands on the line. At the same time, tap your left toe lightly on the ground behind the line.

Advanced Toe Tap

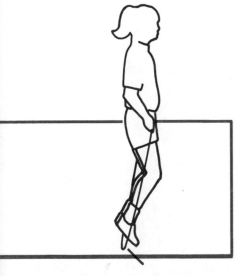

The Advanced Toe Tap leaves out all of the Two-Foot Bounces in the Toe Tap.

Bounce on your left foot while you tap your right toe behind, then bounce on your right foot while you tap your left toe behind, and so on.

Continue by bouncing with both feet together, tapping right toe behind, bouncing feet together, tapping left toe behind, and so on.

Did you remember to warm up?

31

Heel-Toe Tap

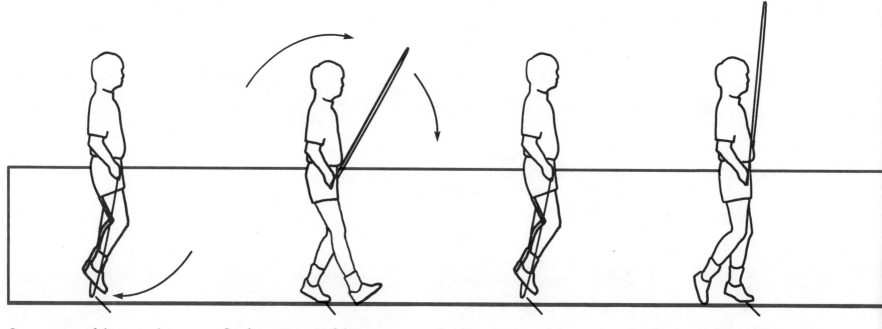

On one turn of the rope, bounce with both feet together on your base line.

On the next turn of the rope, bounce so that your left foot lands on the line. At the same time, tap your right heel lightly on the ground in front of the line.

On the next turn of the rope, bounce with both feet together on the line.

On the next turn of the rope, bounce so that your left foot lands on the line again. At the same time, tap your right toe lightly on the ground behind the line.

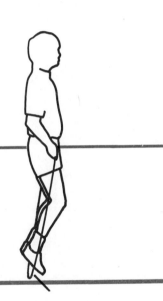

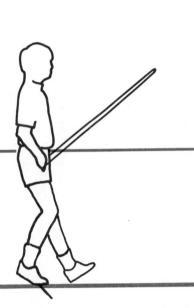

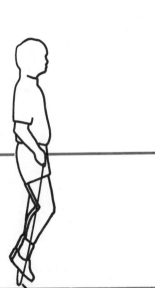

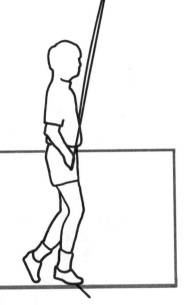

On the next turn of the rope, bounce with both feet together on the line.

On the next turn of the rope, bounce so that your right foot lands on the line. At the same time, tap your left heel lightly on the ground in front of the line.

On the next turn of the rope, bounce with both feet together on the line.

On the next turn of the rope, bounce so that your right foot lands on the line again. At the same time, tap your left toe lightly on the ground behind the line. Continue with this sequence: Two-Foot Bounce, tap right heel, Two-Foot Bounce, tap right toe, Two-Foot Bounce, tap left heel, Two-Foot Bounce, tap left toe, and so on.

Side Step

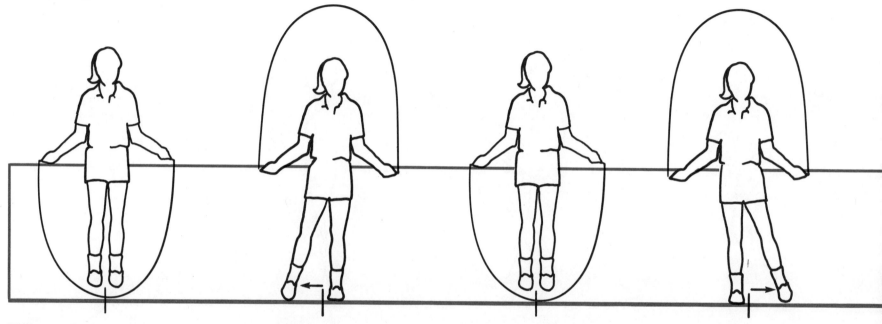

Turn your body so that your base line is between your feet.

On one turn of the rope, bounce with both feet together on top of the line.

On the next turn of the rope, bounce on your left foot. At the same time, tap your right toe lightly on the ground farther out to the right of the line.

On the next turn of the rope, bounce with both feet together on top of the line.

On the next turn of the rope bounce on your right foot. At the same time, tap your left toe lightly on the ground, farther out to the left of the line.

Advanced Side Step

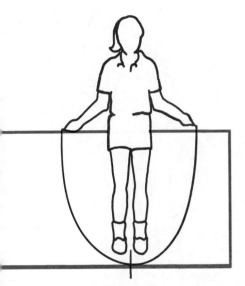

The Advanced Side Step leaves out all of the Two-Foot Bounces in the Side Step.

That means that you bounce on your left foot while tapping your right toe to your right side, then bounce on your right foot while tapping your left toe to your left side, and so on.

Continue by bouncing with feet together, tapping right toe to your right, bouncing with feet together, tapping left toe to your left, and so on.

Practise each new trick without your rope until you can do it well — then try it while jumping over your rope.

Slalom

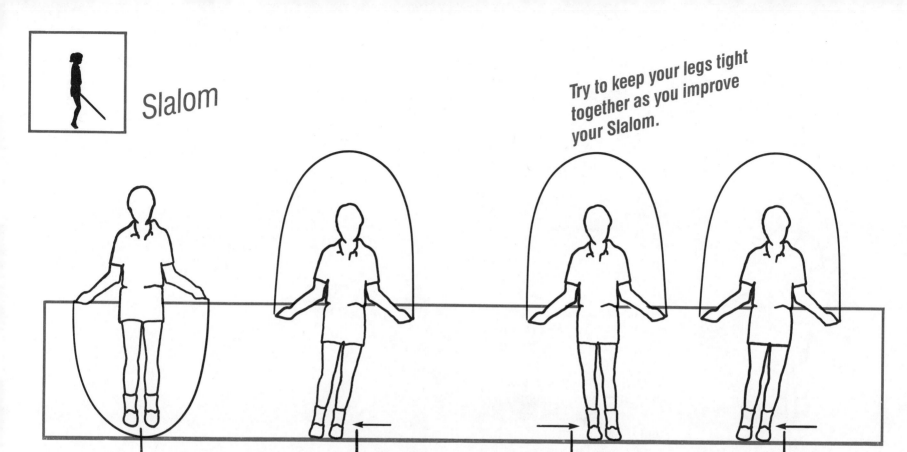

Try to keep your legs tight together as you improve your Slalom.

Turn your body so that the base line is between your feet. On one turn of the rope, bounce with both feet together on top of the line.

On the next turn of the rope, bounce with both feet together so that you land with your feet to the right of the line.

On the next turn of the rope, bounce with both feet together so that you land with your feet to the left of the line.

Continue by bouncing with your feet together to the right, then feet together to the left, and so on.

Jumping Jax

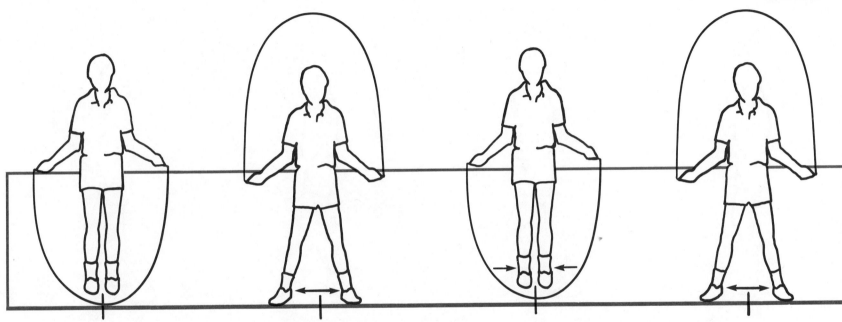

Turn your body so that the base line is between your feet. On one turn of the rope, bounce with both feet together on top of the line.

On the next turn of the rope, bounce and land with your feet wide apart, straddling the line.

On the next turn of the rope, bounce with your feet together.

Continue by bouncing with your feet apart, then together, apart, and so on.

Front-and-Back Jumping Jax

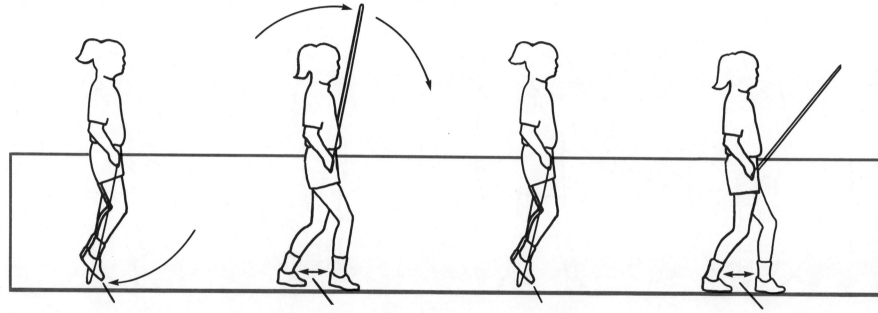

On one turn of the rope, bounce with both feet together on your base line.

On the next turn of the rope, bounce on both feet, but land with your right foot in front of the line while your left foot is behind the line. Your weight should be evenly placed on both feet.

On the next turn of the rope, bounce with both feet together on the line.

On the next turn of the rope, bounce on both feet, but land with your left foot in front of the line and your right foot behind the line. Again, your weight is evenly placed on both feet.

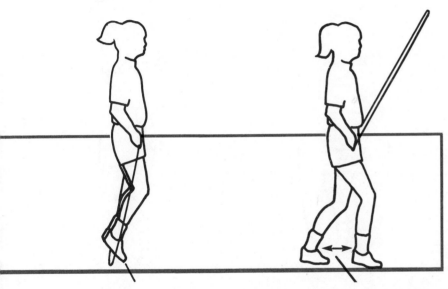

Make sure your rope is the proper length.

On the next turn of the rope, bounce with both feet together on the line.

Continue by bouncing with your right foot in front of the line and the left foot behind, then both feet together, and so on.

Combined Jumping Jax

This trick combines the Front-Jumping Jax with the Front-and-Back Jumping Jax.

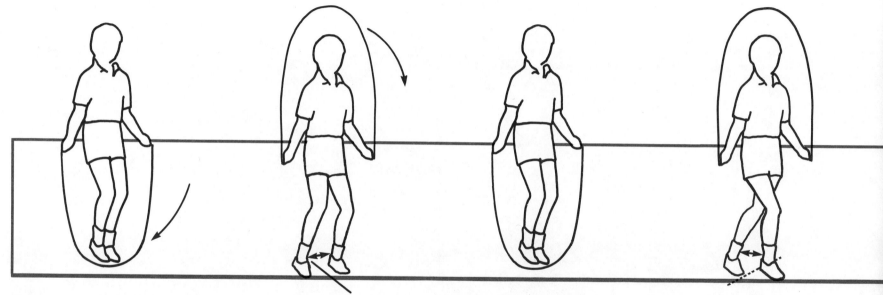

On one turn of the rope, bounce with both feet together.

On the next turn of the rope, bounce and land with your feet apart in a wide straddle.

On the next turn of the rope, bounce with both feet together.

On the next turn of the rope, bounce and land with your right foot forward and your left foot behind.

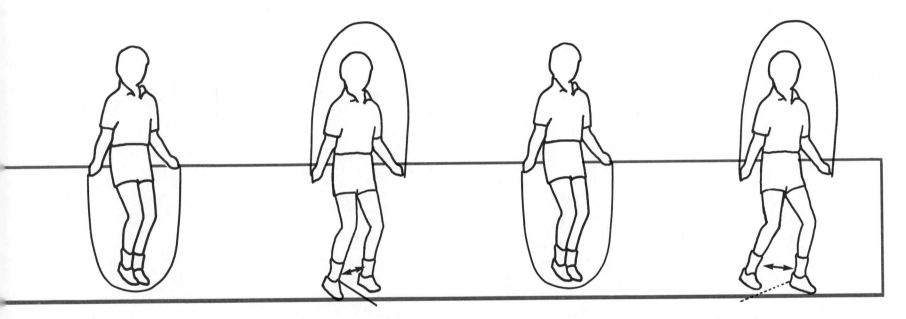

On the next turn of the rope, bounce with both feet together.

On the next turn of the rope, bounce and land with your feet apart in a wide straddle.

On the next turn of the rope, bounce with both feet together.

Continue to bounce with your left foot forward while your right foot is behind, then with feet together, feet apart (straddle), and so on.

X-It

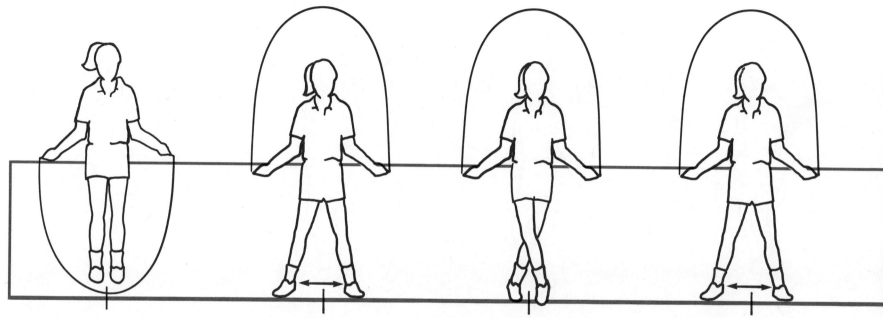

Turn your body so that the base line is between your feet. On one turn of the rope, bounce with both feet together, on top of the line.

On the next turn of the rope, bounce and land with your feet apart, straddling the line.

On the next turn of the rope, bounce and land on both feet, your knees slightly bent, but with your right foot crossing in front and to the left of the line while your left foot crosses behind and to the right of the line.

On the next turn of the rope, bounce and land with your feet apart in a wide straddle.

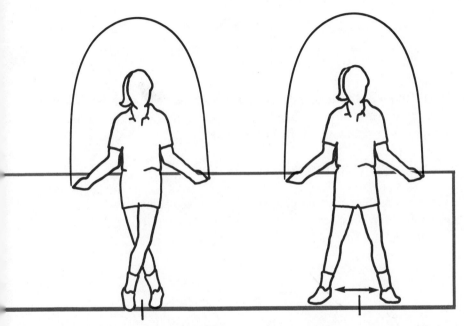

On the next turn of the rope, bounce and land on both feet, with your knees slightly bent, but with your left foot crossing in front and to the right of the line while your right foot crosses behind and to the left of the line.

Continue by bouncing and landing with your feet apart, then crossed right in front of left, then apart, then crossed left in front of right, and so on.

Warm up before you start to skip and cool down after-wards.

A Routine, or Putting It Together

Try your routine to music.

Try your routine beside a friend who can also do the steps.

By this point in, you must be feeling quite proud of yourself. You've learned some basic steps and your feet — and your rope — are moving together in a comfortable skipping rhythm. Now you're ready to be creative, to try to put together the steps you have learned into a simple routine.

For a beginner routine, it is a good idea to repeat each trick four times. Remember that for each of these tricks, you must complete the footwork or the arm action on the left side as well as the right.

You'll find it easier to remember your routine if you start each new trick on the right side. To establish the rhythm of your skipping, always begin with eight Two-Foot Bounces.

Practise any routine first without your rope.

Here's a beginner routine you can try. First do eight Two-Foot Bounces, then four Slaloms, then four X-Its, then four Advanced Side Steps, and finally four Jumping Jax.

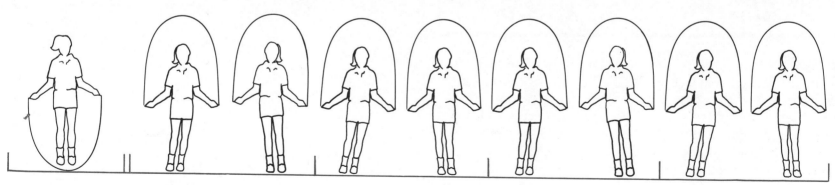

8 Two-Foot
Bounces

4 Slaloms

4 X-Its

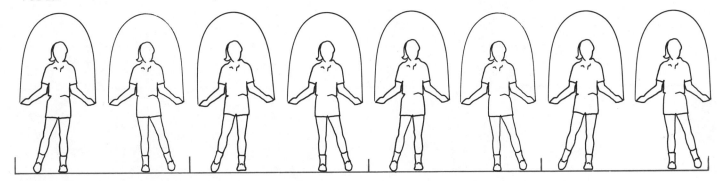

4 Advanced Side Steps

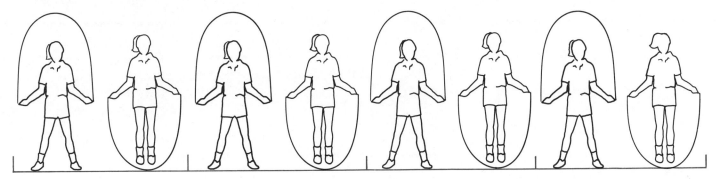

4 Jumping Jax

More Easy Tricks
High Stepping

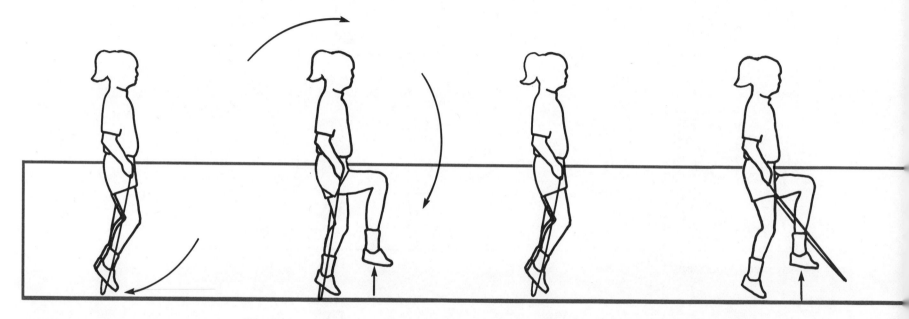

On one turn of the rope, bounce with both feet together.

On the next turn of the rope, bounce on your left foot. At the same time, raise your right knee upward as high as you can.

On the next turn of the rope, bounce with both feet together.

On the next turn of the rope, bounce on your right foot. At the same time, raise your left knee upward as high as you can.

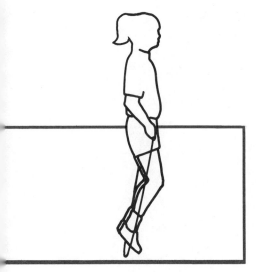

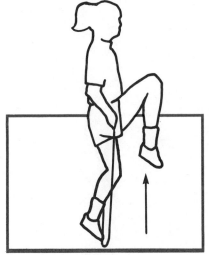

Remember to put your heels down sometimes!

Continue with this sequence: bounce with your feet together, bounce on your left foot while raising your right knee, bounce with your feet together, bounce on your right foot while raising your left knee, and so on.

As your High Stepping improves, try to raise your knee above the height of your waist.

Kick Step

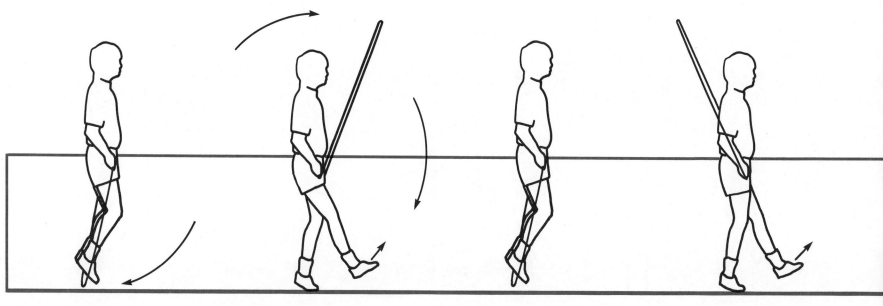

On one turn of the rope, bounce with both feet together.

On the next turn of the rope, bounce on your left foot. At the same time, kick your right foot forward and upward.

On the next turn of the rope, bounce with both feet together.

On the next turn of the rope, bounce on your right foot. At the same time, kick your left foot forward and upward.

Advanced Kick Step

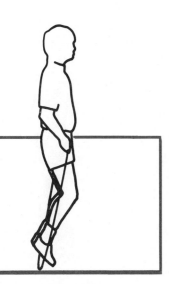

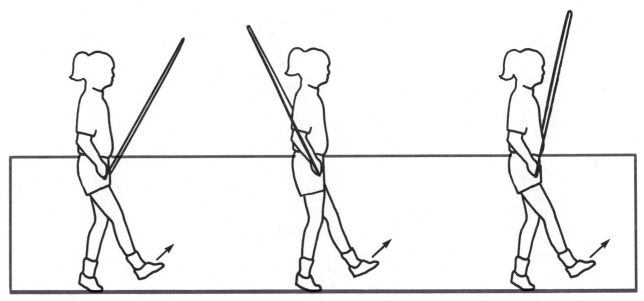

Continue with this sequence: bounce with your feet together, then kick your right foot, feet together, kick your left foot, and so on. Work at kicking higher than your waist!

On one turn of the rope, bounce on your left foot. At the same time, kick your right foot forward and upward.

On the next turn of the rope, bounce on your right foot. At the same time, kick your left foot forward and upward.

Continue by bouncing on your left foot while you kick your right foot, then bouncing on your right foot while you kick your left foot, and so on.

Multi Kicks

Remember to first try new steps without using your rope.

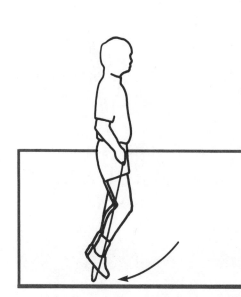 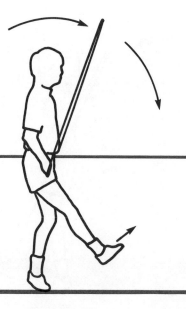 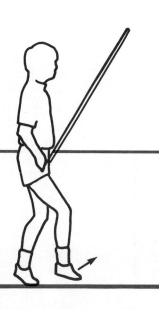 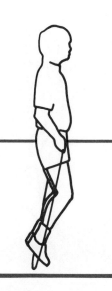

On one turn of the rope, bounce with both feet together.

On the next turn of the rope, bounce on your left foot. At the same time, kick your right foot forward and upward.

On the next turn of the rope, bounce again on your left foot. At the same time, do a little kick with your right foot again. Now you've done two kicks in a row — the first higher than the second.

On the next turn of the rope, bounce with both feet together.

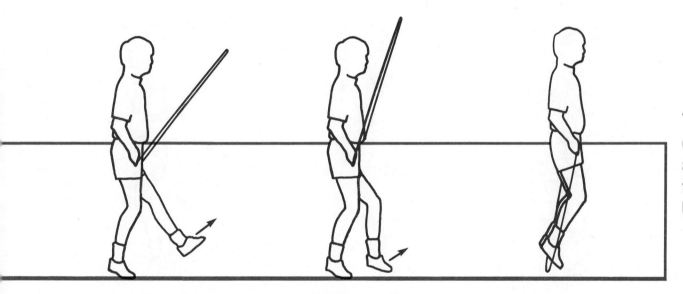

Try other kick combinations—bounce and kick right, left, then two right, then two left. Use your imagination!

On the next turn of the rope, bounce on your right foot. At the same time, kick your left foot forward and upward.

On the next turn of the rope, bounce on your right foot again. At the same time, do a little kick with your left foot again.

Continue with this sequence: bounce with your feet together, bounce twice on your left foot while kicking your right foot twice, bounce with feet together, and so on.

Cancan

Remember to practise without your rope first. This step is tricky to do and you'll need to work at it for a while!

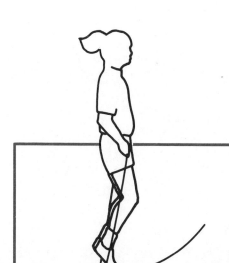

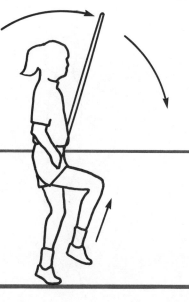

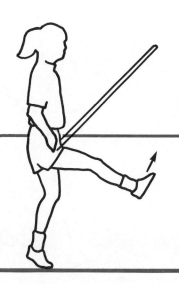

On one turn of the rope, bounce with both feet together.

On the next turn of the rope, bounce on your left foot. At the same time, raise your right knee upward (see High Stepping on page 46).

On the next turn of the rope, bounce with both feet together.

On the next turn of the rope, bounce on your left foot again. At the same time, kick your right foot forward and upward (see the Kick Step on page 48). Keep your right leg straight while you kick.

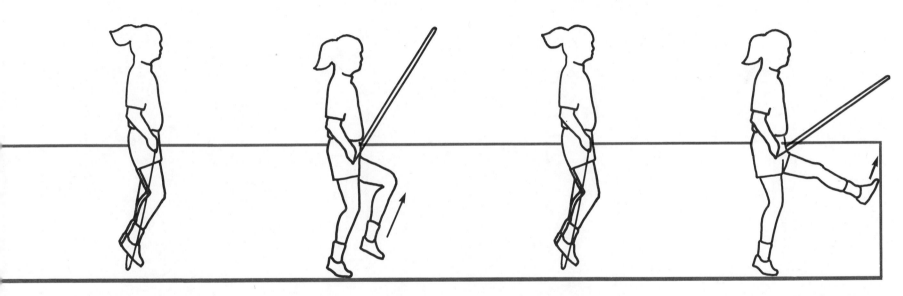

As your Cancan improves, raise your knee and kick your leg as high as you can!

On the next turn of the rope, bounce with both feet together.

On the next turn of the rope, bounce on your right foot. At the same time, raise your left knee upward.

On the next turn of the rope, bounce with both feet together.

On the next turn of the rope, bounce on your right foot again. At the same time, kick your left foot forward and upward. Keep your left leg straight while you kick. Continue with this sequence: bounce with feet together, raise right knee, feet together, kick right foot with leg straight, and so on.

Half Twister

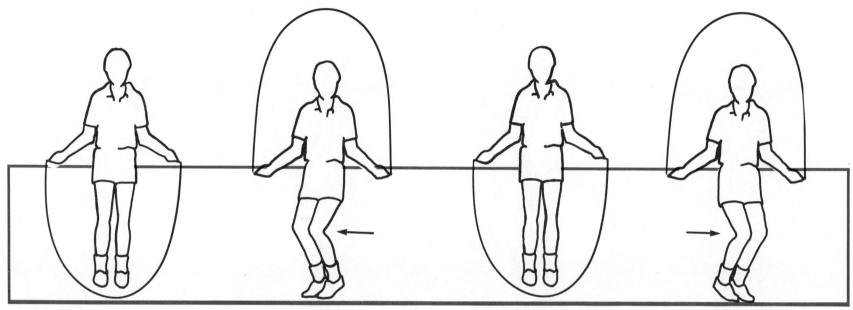

On one turn of the rope, bounce with both feet together.

On the next turn of the rope, bounce with both feet together, but at the same time twist your lower body (hips and legs) to your right and finish your bounce in this position. Your upper body continues to face forward.

On the next turn of the rope, bounce with both feet together, facing forward (in your usual position).

On the next turn of the rope, bounce with both feet together, but at the same time twist your lower body (legs and hips) to your left and finish your bounce in this position. Your upper body continues to face forward. Continue with this sequence: bounce facing forward, then twist right, forward, twist left, and so on.

Full Twister

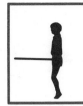

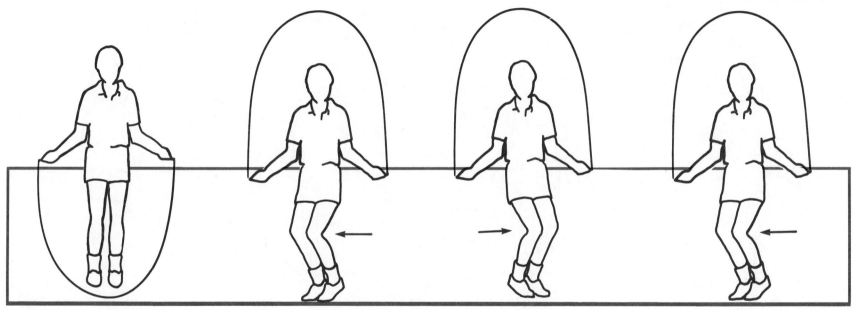

The Full Twister eliminates the forward-facing bounce in the Half Twister.

On one turn of the rope, bounce with both feet together.

On the next turn of the rope, twist to the right as you did in the Half Twister on page 54.

On the next turn of the rope, twist to the left. Continue by twisting to the right, left, right, and so on.

Try staying in the right twist position as you skip a few times.

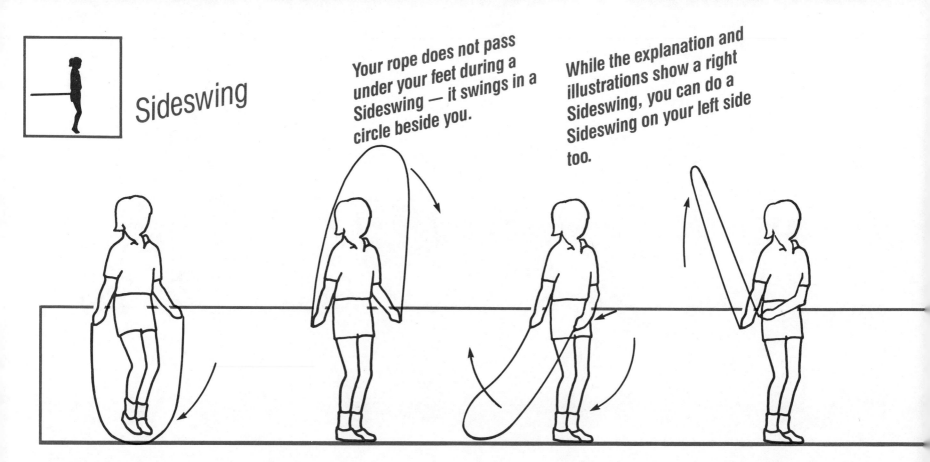

Sideswing

Your rope does not pass under your feet during a Sideswing — it swings in a circle beside you.

While the explanation and illustrations show a right Sideswing, you can do a Sideswing on your left side too.

On one turn of the rope, bounce with both feet together.

Just after you land on the ground, your rope will be overhead and moving forward.

As the rope moves downward in front of you, bring your left hand across toward your right hand.

Keep your hands very close together (with the left hand a little above the right hand) as your rope swings in an upward circle on your right side.

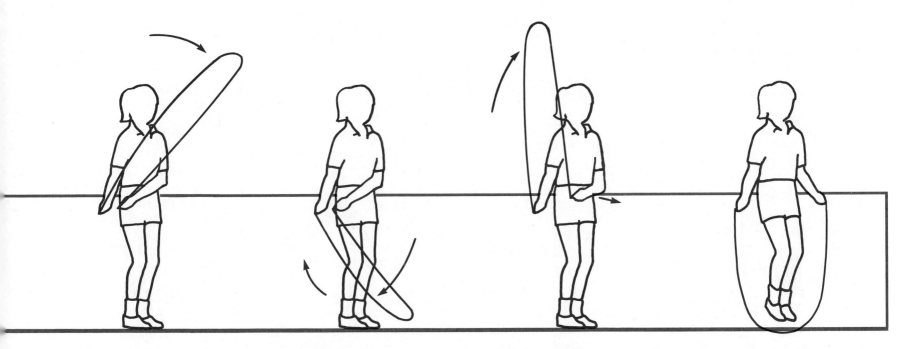

As your hands remain in this position, the rope will swing in a complete circle,

making one Sideswing (on the right side).

To begin skipping again, wait until the rope is at your side, but high over your right shoulder. Bring your left hand back to your left side (in the usual position). The rope will still be moving forward.

Bounce over the rope with both feet together.

Double Sideswing

A Double Sideswing is a Sideswing done first on one side and then on the other side. You do not jump over the rope.

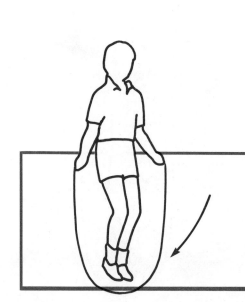   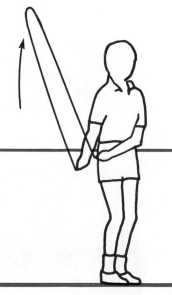

On one turn of the rope, bounce with both feet together.

Just after you land on the ground, your rope will be overhead and moving forward.

Bring your left hand across to your right side to do a Sideswing on your right.

During the right Sideswing, just as the rope is high in the air

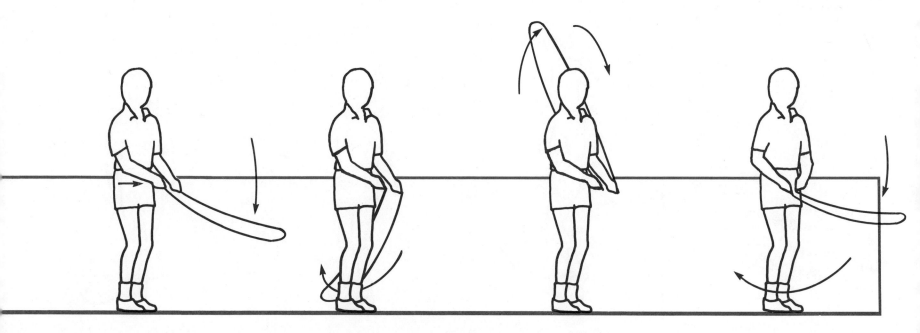

above your right shoulder, move your hands (still close together) to your left side.

Now, with your hands on your left side, complete a Sideswing on the left. Now your right hand is a little above your left hand.

As the rope is high above your left shoulder, you may wish to swing the rope to your right and complete more

Double Sideswings, or you may wish to bring your right hand back to its usual position and skip.

Forward-to-Backwards Half Round

When you "pivot," you turn your body around on the spot so that you end up facing the opposite direction. As you pivot, your rope changes from a forward to a backwards direction.

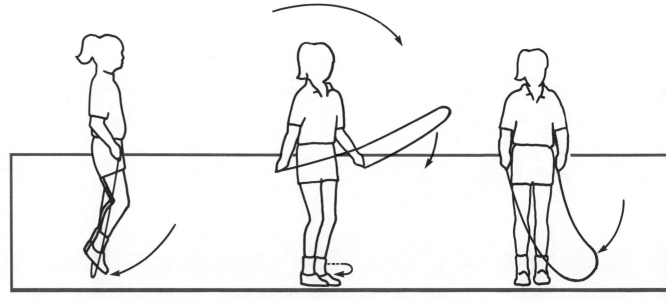

On one turn of the rope, bounce with both feet together.

Just after you land on the ground, the rope will be overhead. When the rope begins to come down (forward) in front of you, begin a Sideswing to your right. At the same time, move both feet toward your right as you pivot on the spot. Keep your hands in their usual position as you do this entire trick.

Continue to turn toward your right. As the rope hits the ground, you will have turned a quarter of the way around.

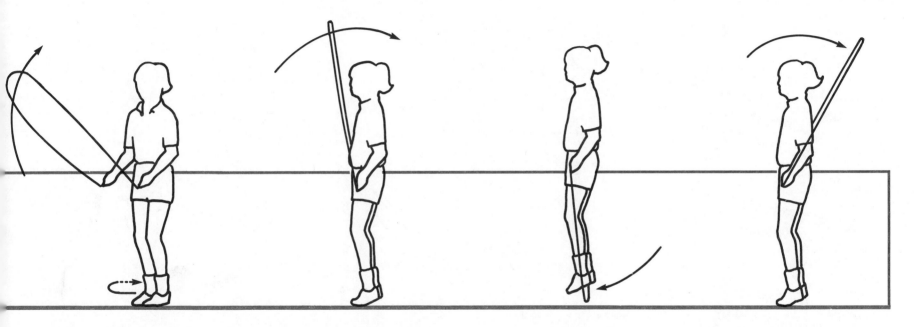

Keep pivoting toward your right as the rope moves in an upward direction from the ground.

You will have pivoted halfway around just as your rope is over-head. Your hands are in their usual rope-turning position. The rope is now moving backwards, even though you have not changed the direction of your rope!

Do a Two-Foot Bounce while the rope moves backwards.

Continue to skip backwards.

Backwards-to-Forward Half Round

Your body starts out facing backwards and, as your rope changes to a forward direction, your body ends up facing forward too.

The rope doesn't really make a turn around you in this trick.

While you turn half way around, your rope should not go over your head. The rope will go backwards under your feet, then move in an upward direction, seem to pause in the air (but not go over your head), then move downward.

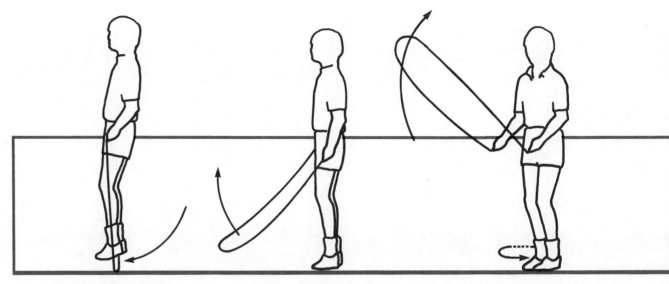

On one turn of the rope, bounce with both feet together while your rope is moving backwards.

After the rope passes under your feet, begin to pivot toward your left.

As you pivot, bring your arms upward to about waist height. Your hands should stay in their usual position at your sides.

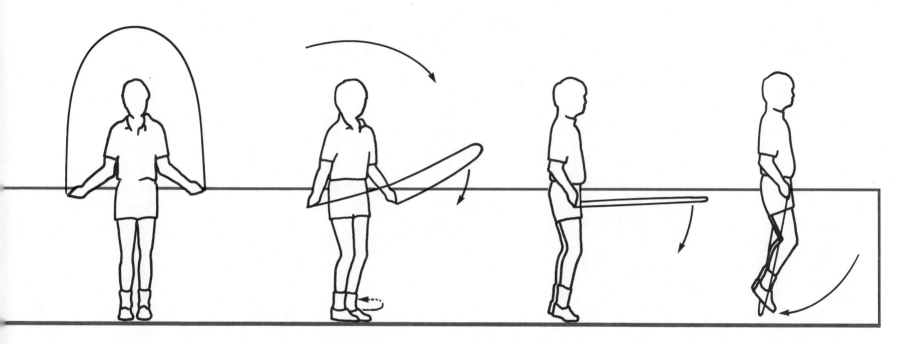

By the time the rope is high in *front* of you, your feet will have turned a quarter of the way around. *Do not let the rope go over your head.* Keep the rope in front of your eyes.

As you continue to turn your feet, start to bring the rope forward and downward.

When you have pivoted halfway around, the rope will be turning forward and downward toward your feet.

Bounce with both feet together over your rope. You are now skipping in a forward direction.

All Round

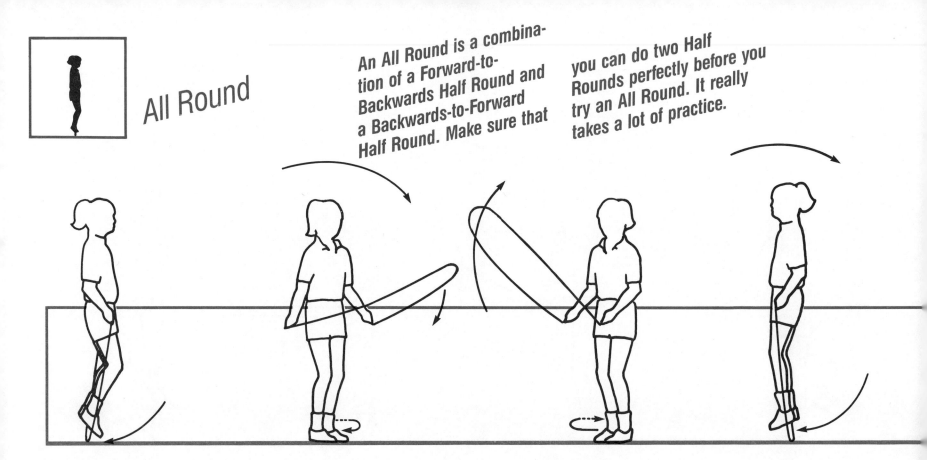

An All Round is a combination of a Forward-to-Backwards Half Round and a Backwards-to-Forward Half Round. Make sure that you can do two Half Rounds perfectly before you try an All Round. It really takes a lot of practice.

On one turn of the rope, bounce with both feet together.

Just as the rope passes over your head, begin a Sideswing to your right. At the same time, pivot your feet toward your right. You are now doing a Forward-to-Backwards Half Round. Continue until you are half way around.

Now, as your rope is turning backwards, bounce with both feet together. You have now completed one Forward-to-Backwards Half Round.

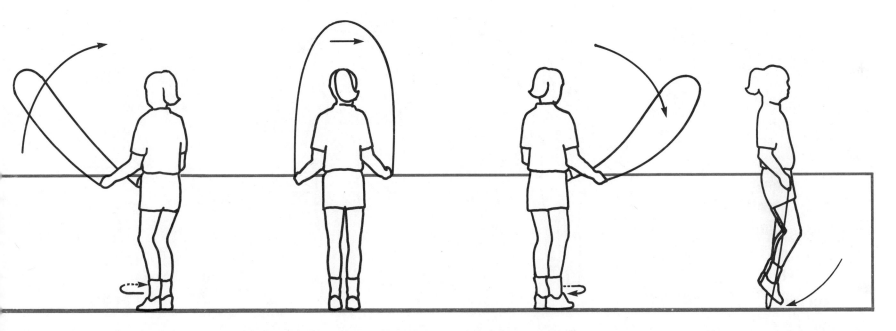

Just after the rope passes under your feet, begin to pivot your feet toward the right again as you start the second Half Round. (Now you're going from backwards to forward.)

Continue to pivot toward your right until you have completed the All Round!

Your rope is now moving forward and downward. Bounce with both feet together.

You may want to do a Half Round to your right and then a Half Round to your left.

If you're having trouble, try one Half Round, then skip four times (backwards), and then complete the second Half Round (which will bring you all the way around).

Forward Cross

Hints: Practise the arm action without the rope first. Then practise the crossing action with your rope, but don't jump over it yet.

Most people have trouble if they don't cross their arms in the right position. Make sure that your arms cross at your elbows and the rope handles point out from your sides. If you don't do this, the loop of the rope will not be wide enough for your body to pass through as you turn the rope in the Cross position.

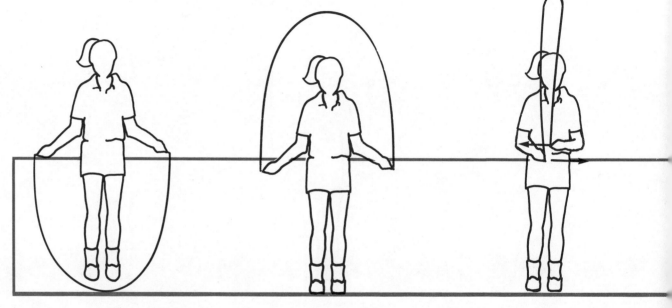

On one turn of the rope, bounce with both feet together.

As your feet land on the ground, your rope is over your head.

Just as your rope begins to travel downward, quickly cross one arm over the other arm

You may wish to jump the rope a few times, keeping your arms crossed.

so that your arms are in the Cross position while you bounce over the rope with your feet together.

Keep your arms in the Cross position until the rope passes overhead and begins to move downward.

Then quickly uncross your arms and bring them back to the usual position.

Bounce with both feet together.

Backward Cross

Remember to cross your arms at your elbows and make sure that your rope handles point out from your sides in the Cross position.

If you have trouble, refer to the Hints on page 66.

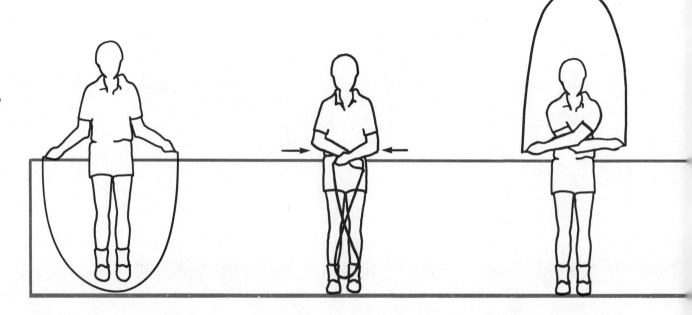

On one *backward* turn of the rope, bounce with both feet together.

Just after the rope passes under your feet, quickly cross one arm over the other arm,

so that your arms are in the Cross position as the rope passes over your head.

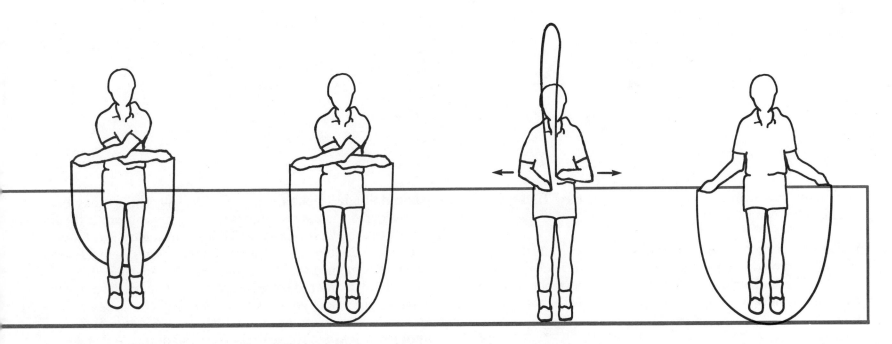

Keep your arms crossed until you bounce over the rope with both feet together.

Just after the rope passes under your feet (while your arms are crossed),

quickly bring your arms back to their usual position.

On the next backward turn of the rope, bounce with both feet together.

You may wish to cross and uncross your arms on each turn of the rope, as shown. You can also keep your arms crossed for a few turns of the rope.

Advanced Tricks
Introduction

Now that you have learned and practised all the Easy Tricks, you are ready to try some harder ones.

There are two sections of Advanced Tricks. It doesn't matter which section you do first — the Advanced Single Tricks or the Combined Tricks. Don't get discouraged if you get tangled in your rope. You may need lots of practice and time to learn these more difficult tricks.

Advanced Single Tricks are on pages 72 to 89. These tricks are also considered basic steps, but are more complicated or difficult than the ones you learned as Easy Tricks. All single tricks (easy ones on pages 25 to 69 and advanced ones on pages 72 to 89) form the basis of combined tricks and routines. The Advanced Single Tricks appear in order of increasing difficulty, so make sure that you master one before going on to the next.

Combined Tricks are single tricks (easy or advanced) that are put together to form a new trick. Usually arm actions from one trick are combined with the footwork of another trick. Here's an example.

If you were to do the X-It with your feet at the same time as you do a Cross with your arms, you would be doing a combined trick. This combined trick is called X-It with a Cross.

Some Reminders

Make sure that you can do all of the Easy Tricks before you try the Advanced Tricks.

Remember to warm up before you skip for at least five minutes and cool down afterwards.

Remember to do at least eight Two-Foot Bounces before you try a new trick step so that you'll feel comfortable with the rhythm of your skipping.

This step is like doing a little dance!

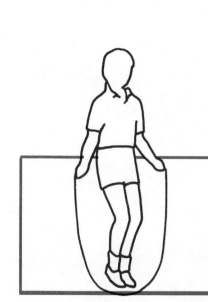  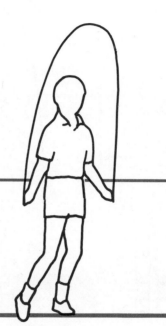 

On one turn of the rope, bounce with both feet together.

On the next turn of the rope, bounce on your left foot. At the same time, tap your right heel forward (see the Heel Tap on page 28).

On the next turn of the rope, bounce on the left foot again. At the same time, tap your right toe to your right side (see the Side Step on page 34).

On the next turn of the rope, bounce on the left foot again. At the same time, raise your right foot upward and to your left so that your right heel is in front of your left knee.

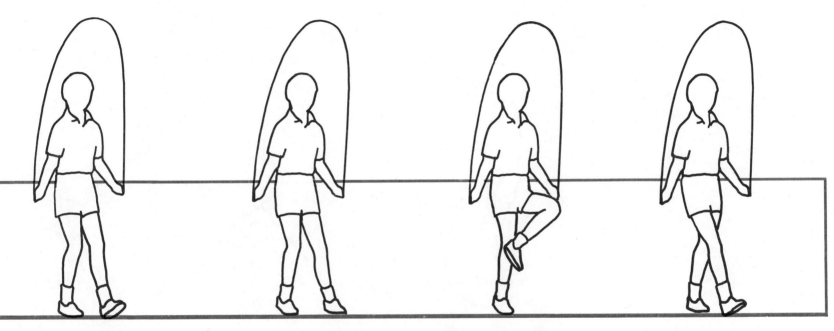

On the next turn of the rope, bounce on your right foot. At the same time, tap your left heel forward.

On the next turn of the rope, bounce on your right foot again. At the same time, tap your left toe to your left side.

On the next turn of the rope, bounce on your right foot again. At the same time, raise your left foot upward and to your right so that your left heel is in front of your right knee.

Continue by bouncing on your left foot while tapping your right heel forward, and so on.

Break It

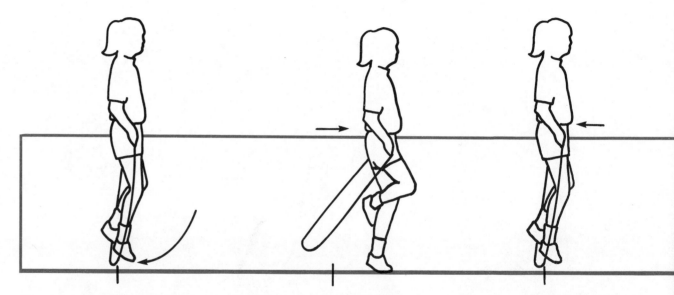

This trick requires some fancy footwork. You don't skip on the spot, but instead travel forward and then backwards while your rope turns in a forward direction. It is very important to first practise the Break It without using your rope!

On one turn of the rope, bounce on your right foot on your base line.

On the next turn of the rope, bounce on your left foot, but move it forward as you bounce in front of your base line. At the same time, bend your right leg at the knee and touch the right heel to the back of the left knee.

In the first part of the sequence, you've moved forward. Now you change your right-foot movements and step backwards.

On the next turn of the rope, bounce on your right foot, but move it back behind you as you bounce on your base line.

74

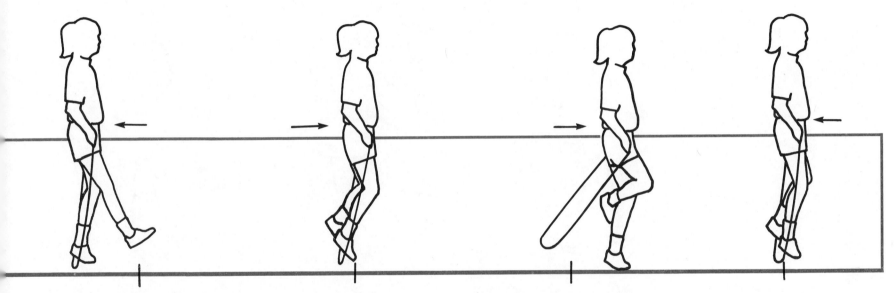

On the next turn of the rope, bounce on your left foot, but move it back one step more behind your base line. At the same time, kick your right foot forward, and upward.

Now repeat the entire sequence. On the next turn of the rope, bounce forward on your right foot on your base line.

On the next turn of the rope, bounce forward in front of your base line onto your left foot while you bend your right leg at the knee and touch the right heel to the back of the left knee.

Continue by bouncing backwards onto your right foot, backwards onto your left as you kick right.

Heel Click

Hint: Begin by bouncing twice on your left foot, then twice on your right, and so on — without your rope. Then, when you feel ready, add the click, so you bounce left, click right, bounce left; bounce right, click left, bounce right, and so on. Finally, try it with your rope!

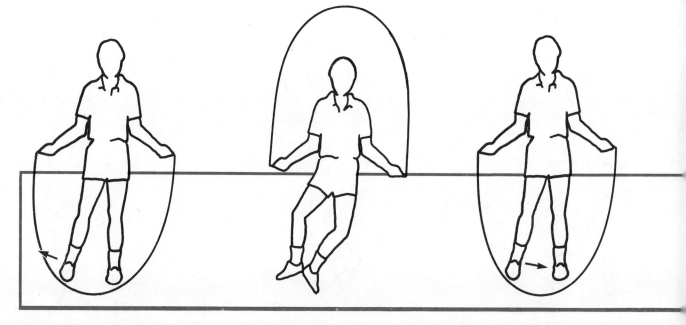

On one turn of the rope, bounce on your left foot. At the same time, keep your right foot towards your right side about 15 cm (six inches) above the ground.

Just after the rope passes under your left foot, land on your left foot. Quickly push off with the left foot and click your heels in the air to your right. (To click your heels, make a very quick up-down action with your right leg just as the left foot comes up to meet it.)

After the click of your heels, the rope passes under your left foot and you land on your left.

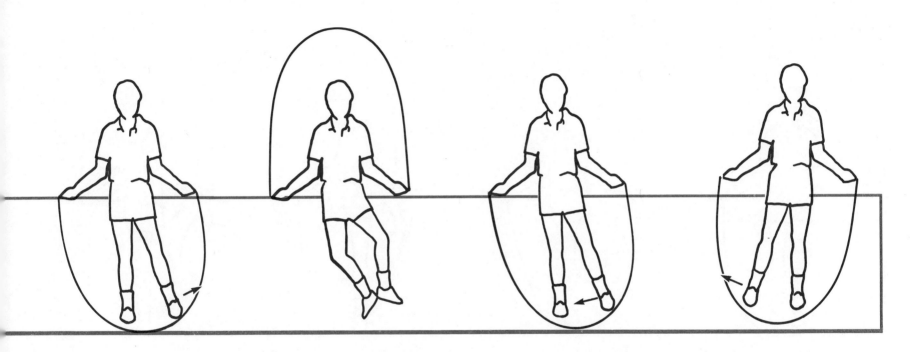

On the next turn of the rope, bounce on your right foot.

Click your heels to your left side while the rope is turning over your head.

Land on your right foot after clicking your heels and after the rope has passed under your right foot.

Continue with this sequence: bounce on your left foot, click to the right, land on left, bounce on right, and so on.

Pretzel

Make sure that your rope handles point out well to the right past your knee, or the rope may catch on your knee as it turns.

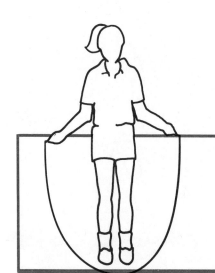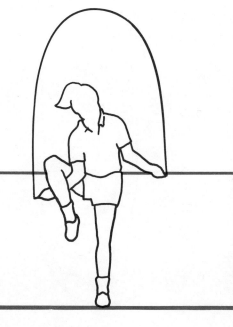

On one turn of the rope, bounce with both feet together.

One the next turn of the rope, bounce on your left foot. At the same time, lift your right knee upward and point it toward your right side, with the right knee behind your right forearm. On the next turn of the rope, bounce in this position again.

On the next turn of the rope, just after the rope passes under your left foot on the bounce, quickly move your right hand behind your right knee.

On the next turn of the rope, bounce on your left foot while staying in the Pretzel position. (You may wish to stay in this position for a few skips.)

You don't bounce over the rope with your left foot to get out of the Pretzel. Instead, just as the rope is about to hit the ground, bring your right hand from under your knee to meet your

left hand. Do a Sideswing to your left side. When the rope is at your side, high over your left

shoulder, bring your right hand back to your right side in the usual position.

Bounce with both feet together.

The Pretzel can also be done by putting your left hand under your left knee. Can you do the Pretzel while skipping backwards?

Down Under

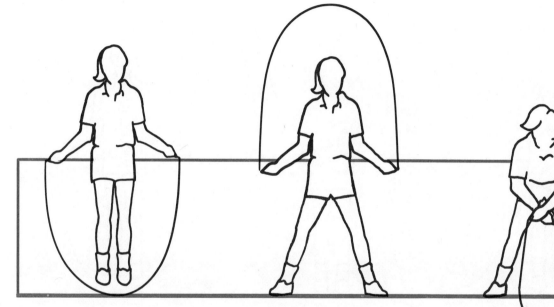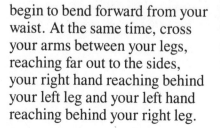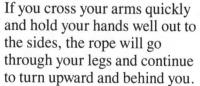

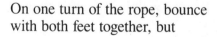On one turn of the rope, bounce with both feet together, but

land with your feet well apart. Just as the rope moves forward and over your head,

begin to bend forward from your waist. At the same time, cross your arms between your legs, reaching far out to the sides, your right hand reaching behind your left leg and your left hand reaching behind your right leg.

If you cross your arms quickly and hold your hands well out to the sides, the rope will go through your legs and continue to turn upward and behind you.

Stay in this Down Under position. The rope will move over your back until

it stops when it lands on the ground. You'll seem tangled! Don't panic — this is correct!

Jump, or step, over the rope which is across your feet.

Bring your hands forward and upward, back to the usual skipping position, and you will now find yourself skipping in a backwards direction.

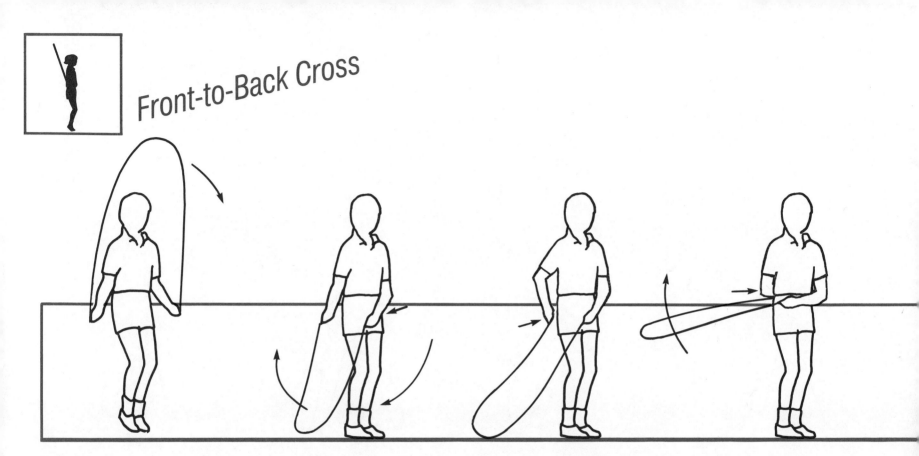

Front-to-Back Cross

On one turn of the rope, bounce with both feet together. Land on both feet. Just as the rope passes over your head, begin to bring

your left hand across to your right as you begin a Sideswing on your right.

As the rope hits the ground on your right during the beginning of the Sideswing, quickly bring your right hand behind your

back so that it crosses to your left side.

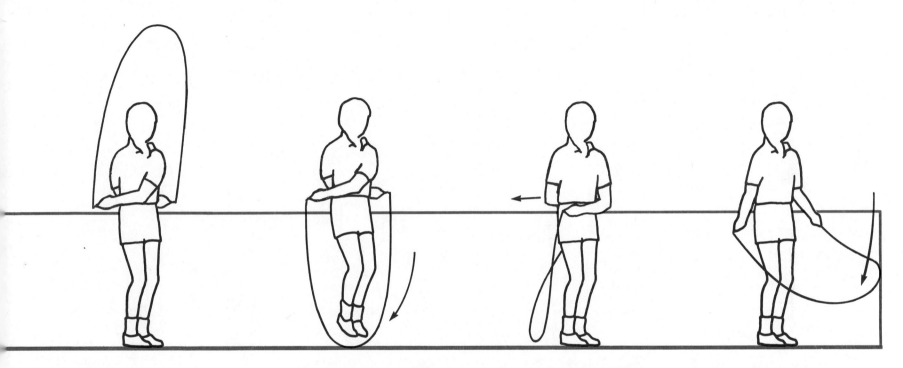

Keep your hands in this Front-to-Back Cross position as the rope passes forward over your head.

Your right arm must be placed behind you, far to the left, so that the rope will turn easily around you without getting caught.

Bounce over the rope, keeping your arms in this position. (You can turn your rope and skip if you wish.)

You can easily get out of the cross position. After you bounce over the rope, bring your arms very quickly back to their usual position.

The rope will continue to turn forward and you can then do a Two-Foot Bounce Step.

Behind-the-Back Cross

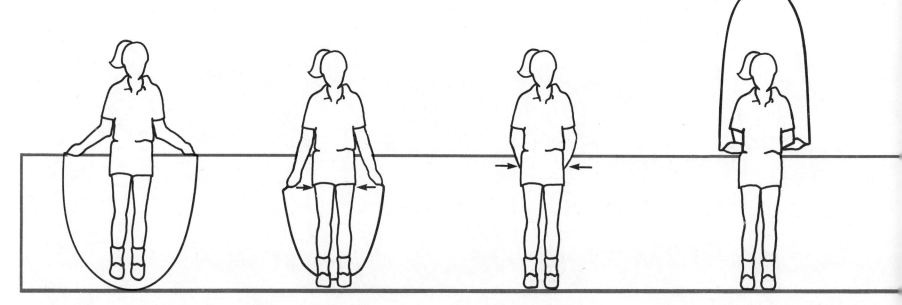

On one turn of the rope, bounce with both feet together.

Just as your feet land on the next turn of the rope, begin to bring your hands behind your back so that

your right hand goes to the left side and your left hand goes to the right side. (The rope continues upward, but it's out of sight for an instant.)

By the time your rope is overhead, your arms should be crossed behind your back. Make sure that your hands and rope are well out to the side so that the loop of the rope will be wide enough to pass over your body as the rope turns.

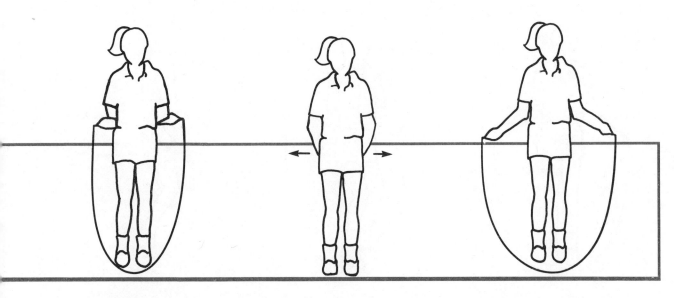

Bounce over the rope with your arms in this cross position. You can get out of the Behind-the-Back Cross just after you bounce over the rope.

Quickly uncross your arms and bring them back to their usual position. The rope continues to turn forward

so that you can jump over the rope with a Two-Foot Bounce.

Spinner

To perform a "spin," you turn your body 360° in the air before you land.

The Spinner is difficult to do. You must jump very high and spin in the air (to your right) all the way around. When you land, you will be facing in the same direction as when you began to jump. As you jump and spin around in the air, your rope turns one time. You land after the spin and just after the rope passes under your feet.

Remember to try it a few times without your rope first!

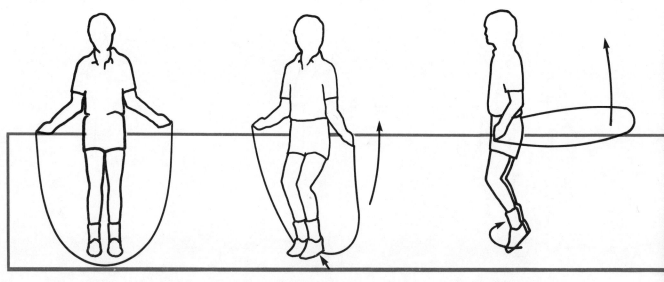

On one turn of the rope, bounce with both feet together.

Just as you land after bouncing over the rope, jump again — as high as you can — and at the same time spin quickly in the air

to your right.

You will reach the highest part of your jump when you have spun halfway around.

Continue to spin to your right as you move downward,

spinning still to your right

with the rope passing under your feet just before you land.

Double Under

In this trick, you must do one very high jump. At the same time, you turn your rope very quickly with your wrists so that it goes under your feet two times before you land.

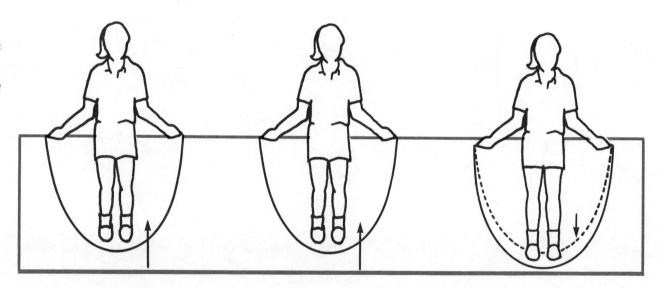

Practise eight Two-Foot Bounces, turning the rope slowly and jumping as high as you can.

On the Double Under, the rope passes under your feet the first time when you are high off the ground,

then passes under your feet the second time just before you land.

Triple Under

If you can jump really high and if you can turn your rope really quickly, then try a Triple Under! The rope goes under your feet three times on one jump.

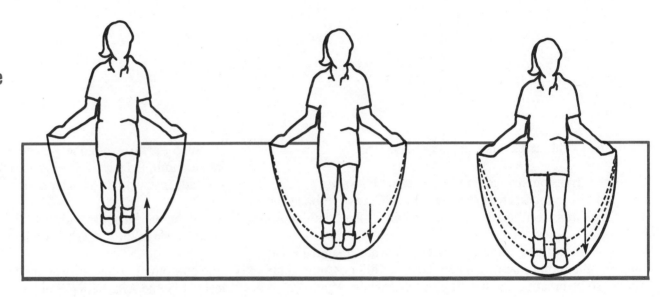

First turn   Second turn   Third turn

Combined Tricks

Combined tricks are single tricks that you put together to make a new trick.

You'll find Combined Tricks on pages 92 to 115.

Combined tricks put arm actions together with footwork. The combinations in this section of the book are Cross combinations, Sideswing Cross combinations, and Double Under combinations.

When you know these combined tricks, use your imagination to make up other combinations. There are over 100 possible combinations, so be creative and try different things!

Because you already know how to do each single trick that goes into a combined trick, the single tricks are not explained in detail. Instead, instructions are given for putting them together.

So, if you have trouble with one of the tricks, go back to the explanation of the single trick and practise it some more.

The combinations use *arm* actions (like the Cross) with *foot* patterns (like the Alternating Step, Kick Step, and so on). Practise the foot patterns so that you can do them really well, then add the arm actions.

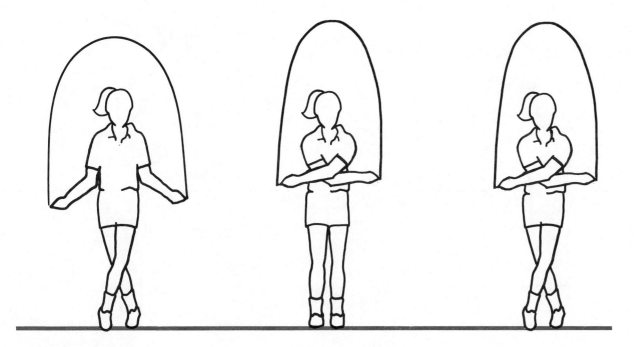

If you were to do the X-It with your feet at the same time as you do
a Cross with your arms, you would be doing a combined trick.
This combined trick is called X-It with a Cross.

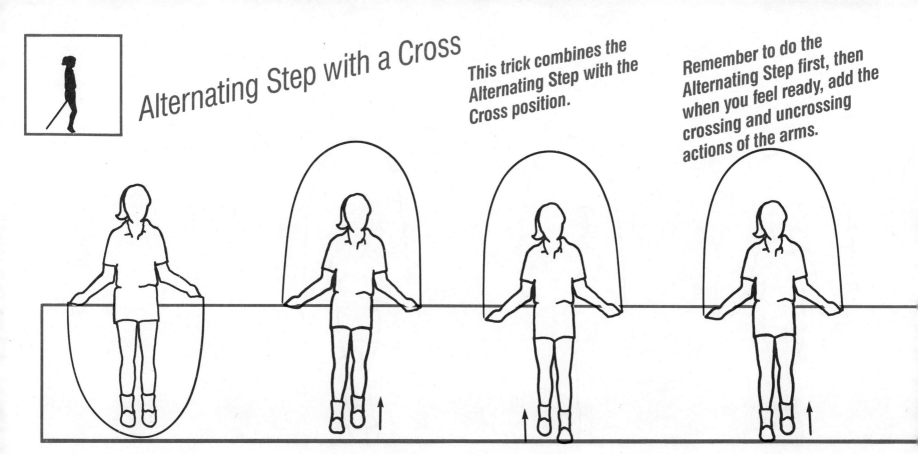

Alternating Step with a Cross

This trick combines the Alternating Step with the Cross position.

Remember to do the Alternating Step first, then when you feel ready, add the crossing and uncrossing actions of the arms.

Do a Two-Foot Bounce.

Bounce on your right foot.

Bounce on your left foot.

Bounce on your right foot.

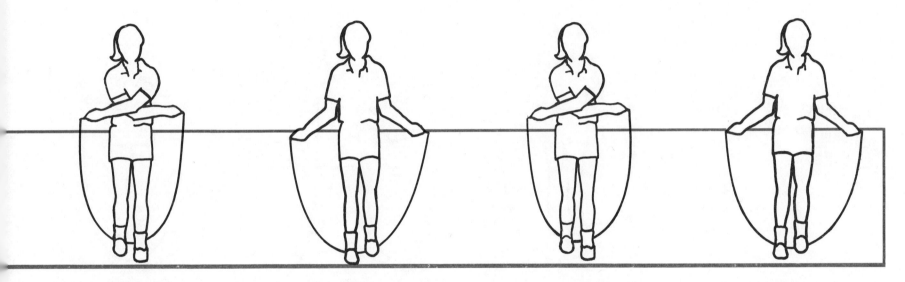

Bounce on your left foot and cross your arms in front of you.

Bounce on your right foot and uncross your arms and go back to the usual skipping position.

Bounce on your left foot and cross your arms in front of you.

Bounce on your right foot and uncross your arms and go back to the usual skipping position. Continue to cross and uncross your arms while alternating your feet.

Jumping Jax with a Cross

This trick combines the Jumping Jax with the Cross position.

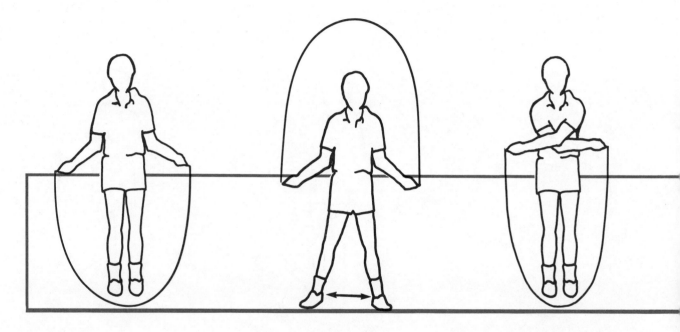

Do a Two-Foot Bounce.

Bounce and land with your feet apart in a wide straddle.

Bounce with your feet together, but with your arms crossed.

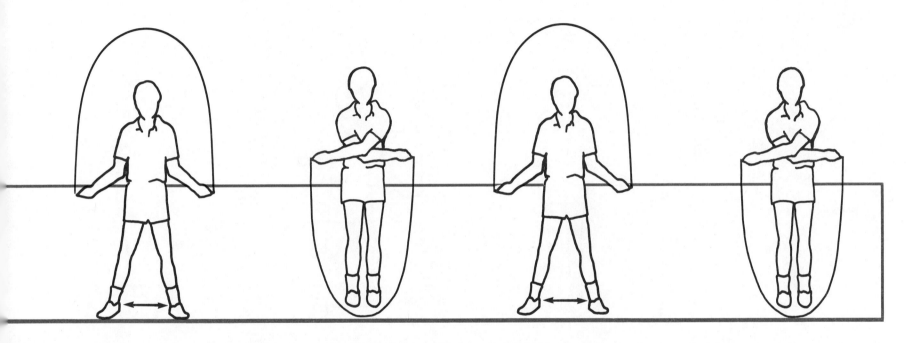

Bounce and land with your feet apart and with your arms uncrossed.

Bounce with your feet together, but with your arms crossed.

Bounce and land with your feet apart and with your arms uncrossed.

Continue to cross your arms while you bounce with your feet together and uncross your arms while you bounce with your feet apart.

X-It with a Cross

This trick combines the X-It with the Cross position.

Remember to begin skipping by first practising the foot pattern. Add the arm actions when you feel ready.

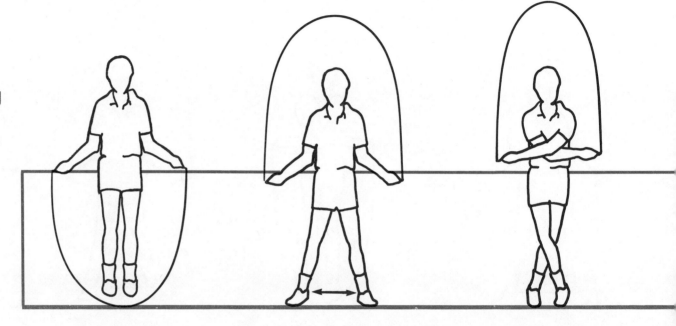

Do a Two-Foot Bounce.

Bounce and land with your feet apart in a wide straddle.

Bounce with your arms crossed and land with your feet in the X position, your right foot in front of your left foot.

Uncross your arms and bounce, landing with your feet apart.

Bounce with your arms crossed and land with your feet in the X position, your left foot in front of your right foot.

Uncross your arms and bounce, landing with your feet apart.

Continue to cross and uncross your arms as you bounce while crossing and uncrossing your feet.

Half Twister with a Cross

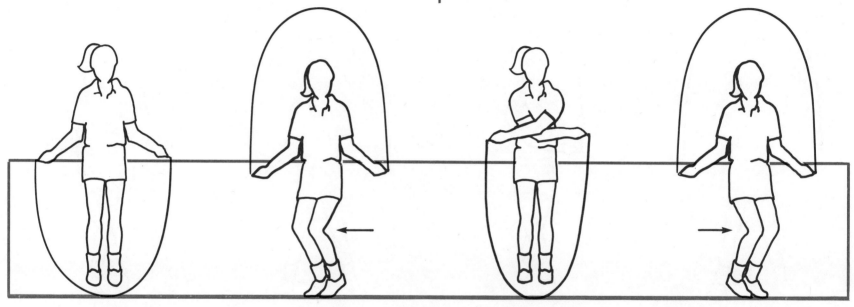

Do a Two-Foot Bounce.

Bounce and twist your lower body (hips and legs) to your right.

Cross your arms as you bounce facing forward.

Uncross your arms as you bounce and twist your lower body (hips and legs) to your left.

Continue with this sequence: cross your arms as you face forward and uncross your arms as you twist right, and so on.

Full Twister with a Cross

This trick combines the Full Twister with the Cross position.

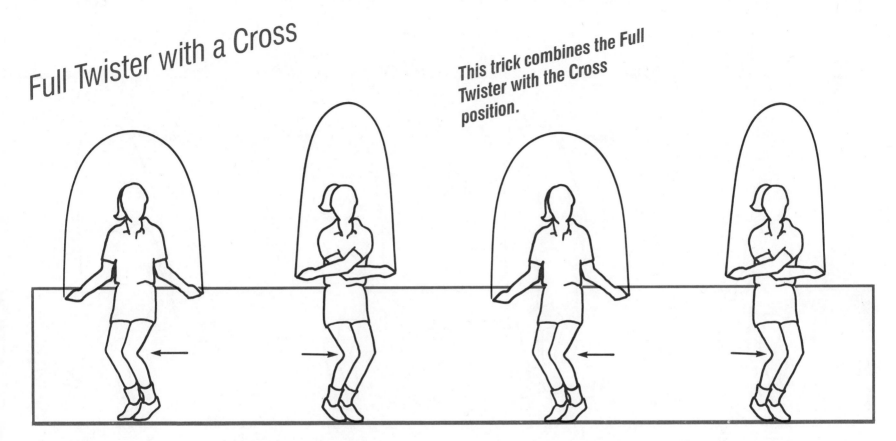

Bounce and twist your lower body to your right.

Bounce with arms crossed and twist your lower body to your left.

Bounce with arms uncrossed and twist your lower body to your right.

Continue with this sequence: cross your arms as you twist left and uncross your arms as you twist right, and so on.

Cancan with a Cross

This trick combines the Cancan with the Cross position.

Note: It is especially important to practise the Cancan before adding your arm cross for this combination!

Do a Two-Foot Bounce.

As you bounce, raise your right knee as high as you can.

Do a Two-Foot Bounce with arms crossed.

Uncross your arms as you bounce and kick your right foot upward, as high as you can.

Do a Two-Foot Bounce with arms crossed.

Uncross your arms as you bounce and raise your left knee as high as you can.

Do a Two-Foot Bounce with arms crossed.

Uncross your arms as you bounce and kick your left foot upward, as high as you can.

Continue to cross and uncross your arms as you bounce, raise your knee, bounce, kick your foot, and so on.

Sideswing with a Cross (Sideswing Cross)

This trick combines the Sideswing with the Cross position.

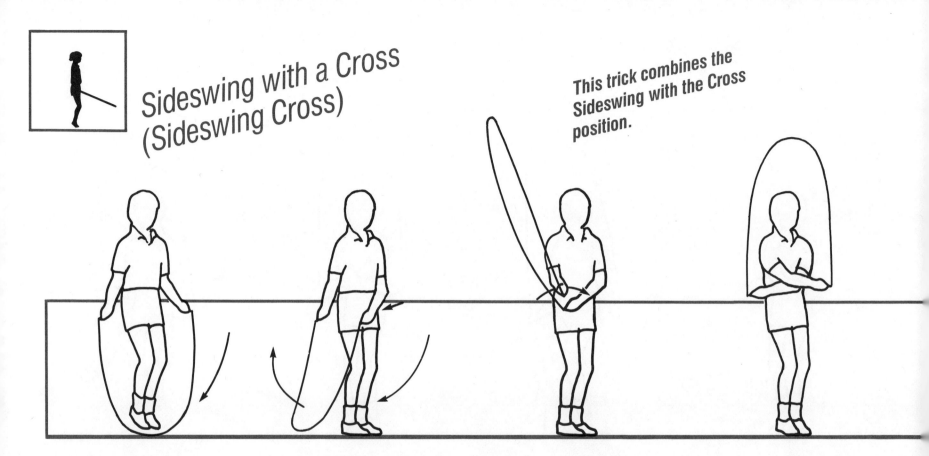

After bouncing and just after the rope passes over your head,

begin to do a Sideswing to your right side.

As the rope passes your right shoulder, bring your right arm over your left arm into the Cross position.

Bounce over the rope in the Cross position.

Remember that you do not jump over the rope in the Sideswing.

Practise the Sideswing with a Cross many times so that you can do it easily and almost without thinking before you add the tricks on pages 104 to 115.

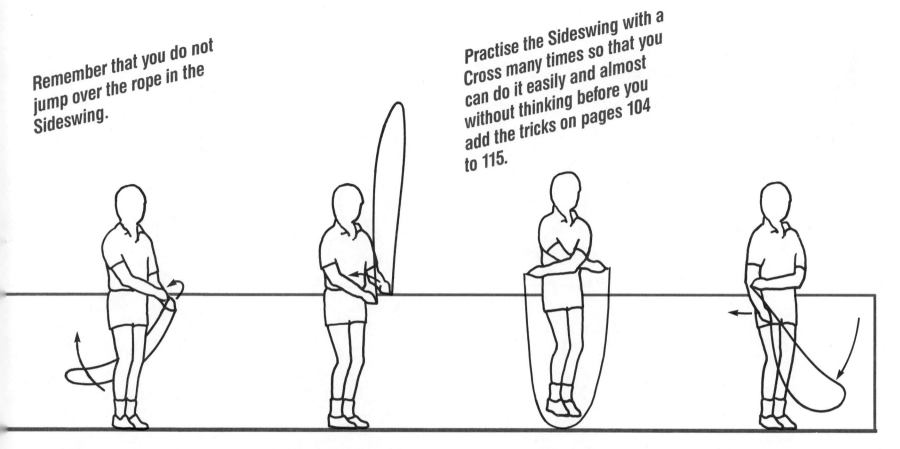

·After bouncing, uncross your left arm from underneath. Keep your right arm across your body. Now do a Sideswing on the left side.

As the rope passes your left shoulder, bring your right arm

into the Cross position. Bounce over the rope.

Continue to do a Sideswing (right), Cross and bounce, Sideswing (left), Cross and bounce, and so on.

Sideswing Cross with an Alternating Step

This trick combines the Sideswing Cross with the Alternating Step.

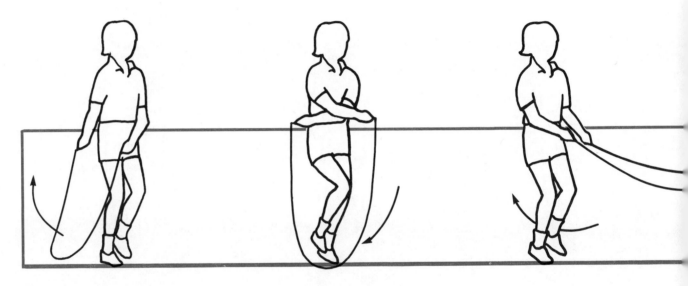

Add a bounce while you do your Sideswing. The rope must go beside you and *not* under your feet.

Do a Sideswing to your right while you bounce on your right foot.

Cross your arms while you bounce on your left foot.

Do a Sideswing on your left while you bounce on your right foot.

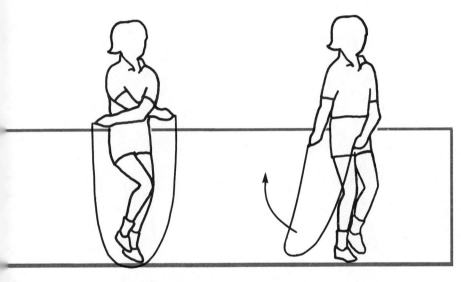

Cross your arms while you bounce on your left foot.

Continue to do a Sideswing, Cross, Sideswing, etc., while you alternate your feet from right, to left, to right, and so on.

Remember to put your heels down sometimes!

Sideswing Cross with a Kick

This trick combines the Sideswing Cross with the Kick Step.

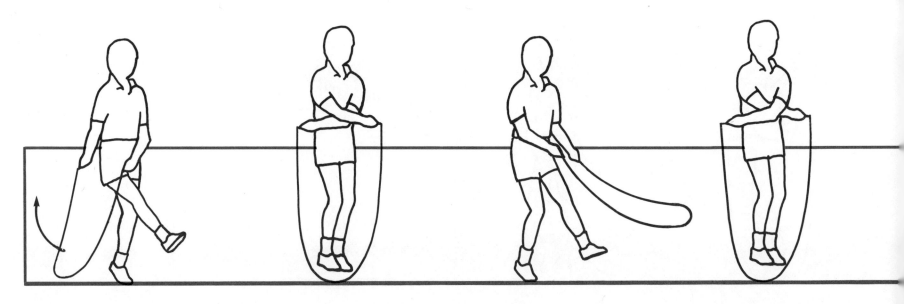

Do a Sideswing to your right while you bounce on your left foot and kick your right foot upward. (Remember that your rope does not go under your foot as you bounce.)

Cross your arms (right over left) while you bounce with both feet together.

Do a Sideswing to your left while you bounce on your right foot and kick your left foot upward.

Cross your arms (left over right) while you bounce with both feet together.

Continue to do a Sideswing to the right, while kicking right, cross arms and bounce, and so on.

You may wish to do the kick on each bounce — or do two right kicks then two left kicks. Use your imagination!

Sideswing Cross with a Heel-Toe Tap

This trick combines the Sideswing Cross with the Heel-Toe Tap.

Remember to begin with the footwork (Heel-Toe Tap) and then when you're ready, add the Sideswing Cross.

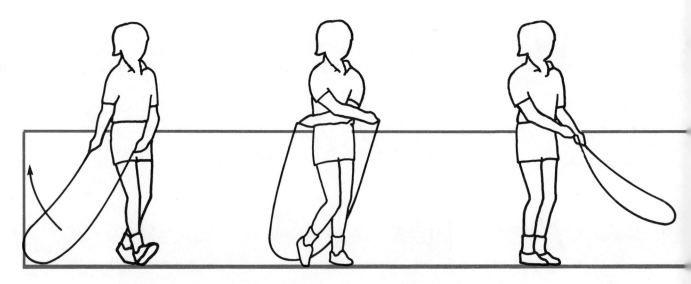

Do a Sideswing to your right as you bounce on your left foot and keep your right heel forward on the ground.

Cross your arms (right over left) as you bounce on your left foot and tap your right toe behind you on the ground.

Do a Sideswing to your left as you bounce with both feet together.

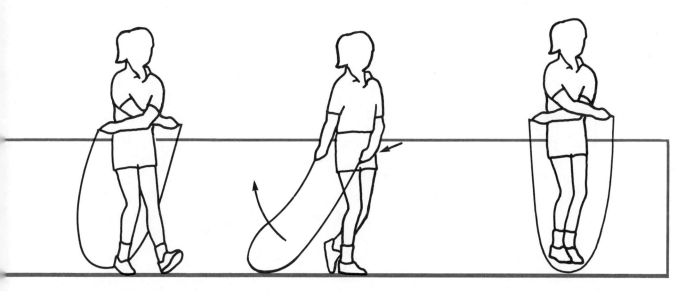

Cross your arms (left over right) as you bounce on your right foot and tap your left heel forward on the ground.

Do a Sideswing to your right as you bounce on your right foot and tap your left toe behind you on the ground.

Continue to do a Cross, Sideswing, Cross, etc., while you bounce with feet together, tap right heel, tap right toe, feet together, tap left heel, tap left toe, and so on.

Try to leave out the Two-Foot Bounce so that you tap heel, toe, heel, toe, etc., as you do a Sideswing, Cross, Sideswing, Cross, and so on.

Sideswing Cross with the Cancan

This trick combines the Sideswing Cross with the Cancan.

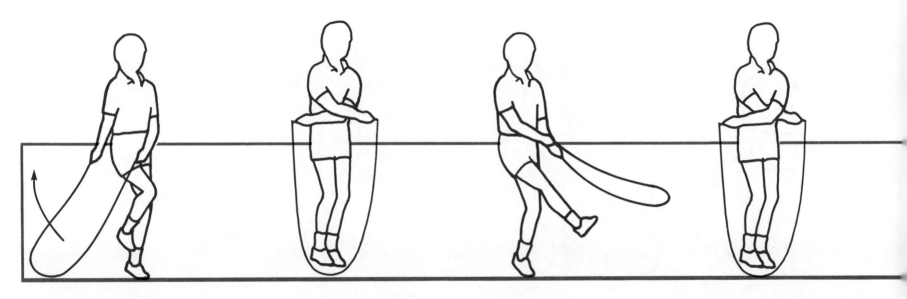

Do a Sideswing to your right as you bounce on your left foot and, at the same time, raise your right knee. (Remember that you don't bounce over the rope when you do the Sideswing.)

Cross your arms (right over left) as you bounce with both feet together.

Do a Sideswing to your left as you bounce on your left foot again, and at the same time kick your right foot upward.

Cross your arms (left over right) as you bounce with both feet together.

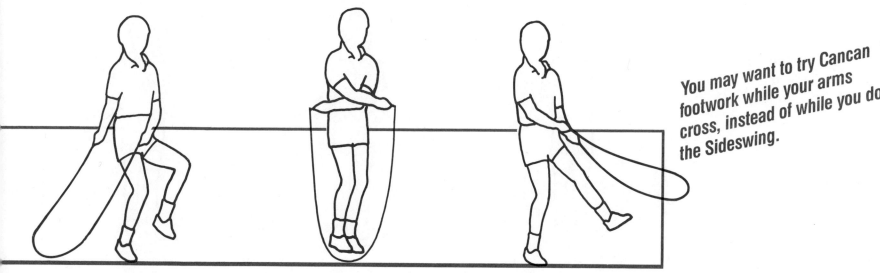

You may want to try Cancan footwork while your arms cross, instead of while you do the Sideswing.

Do a Sideswing to your right as you bounce on your right foot and at the same time raise your left knee.

Cross your arms (right over left) as you bounce with both feet together.

Do a Sideswing to your left as you bounce on your right foot again, and at the same time kick your left foot upward.

Continue to do a Cross, Sideswing, Cross, etc., while you bounce with both feet together, raise knee, feet together, kick leg, feet together, and so on.

111

Double Under with a Two-Foot Bounce

Before combining Double Unders with other tricks, you should first be able to do 20 Double Unders (with a Two-Foot Bounce between each) in a row.

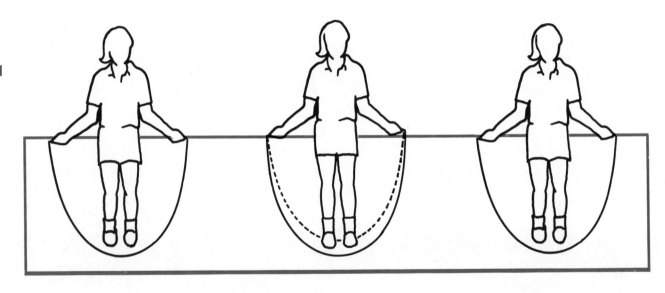

Do one *high* Two-Foot Bounce. (The rope turns once.)

Do a Double Under. (The rope turns twice.)

Do one high Two-Foot Bounce.

Continue to do a Double Under, a Two-Foot Bounce, a Double Under, and so on.
Can you do more than 20?

Continuous Double Unders

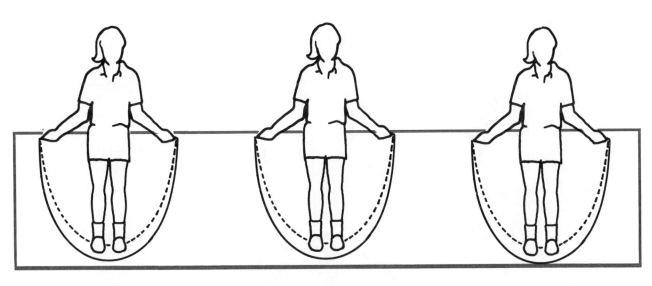

Do a Double Under,   and another Double Under,   and another Double Under.

How many Double Unders can you do in a row?

Some skippers can do more than 100 Double Unders in a row!

Double Under with a Cross

This trick combines the Double Under with the Cross position.

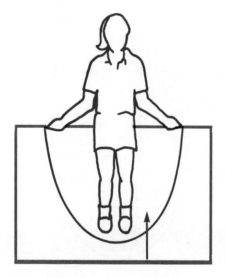

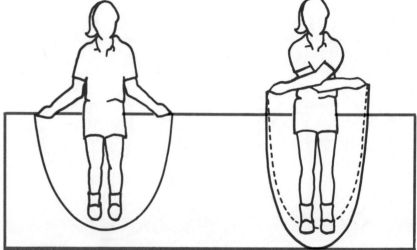

Do one or two high Two-Foot Bounces.

In the Double Under with a Cross, on the first of the two turns of the rope, keep your arms in their usual position.

Quickly cross your arms so the rope completes its second turn before your feet touch the ground. The rope has passed under your feet two times on one high jump.

Double Under with a Sideswing Cross

This trick combines the Double Under with the Sideswing Cross.

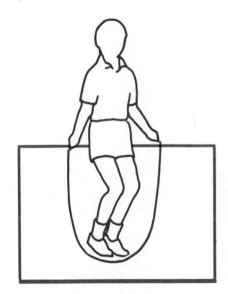

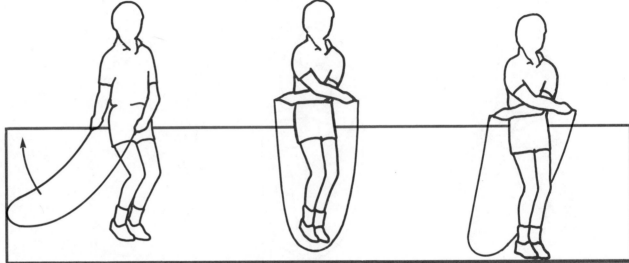

Do one or two high Two-Foot Bounces.

In this trick, as you jump high, on the first turn of the rope, do a fast Sideswing beside you

and then quickly bring your arms to the Cross position so that the rope goes under your feet on this second turn of the rope.

Land just after the rope goes under your feet. The rope has turned twice (once for the Sideswing and again for the Cross) on one high jump.

More Combined Tricks

You can combine tricks in over 100 ways. Use your imagination and make up your own combinations as you become more expert at skipping.

Combined Arm Actions with Footwork

Combine any of the arm crosses with the Heel Tap, Toe Tap, Heel-Toe Tap, Side Step, Slalom, Jumping Jax (three ways), High Stepping, X-It, Kick Step, Cancan, Half and Full Twister, Half Round, Fling, Break It, or Heel Click. Or, combine the Side-swing or the Sideswing Cross with any of those tricks.

Challenge yourself! Once you've mastered a trick in which the rope turns forward, try the same trick with the rope turning backwards.

Add other kinds of footwork or turns to Double or Triple Under combinations. See what you can come up with!

Put a series of single or combined tricks together to music to make more complicated and advanced routines. Travel forward, backwards, or sideways as you perform your tricks or your routine!

Combined Turns with Footwork or Arm Actions

Do a Half Round in the Pretzel position, or a Half Round with some kind of Cross, or a Spinner with a Cross or with a Sideswing Cross.

Partner Skipping Routines

As you have been learning new tricks, you have probably also been putting tricks together in a routine. Now try to compose a routine with a friend. In a partner routine, both you and your partner perform the same tricks at the same time. At first, keep your routine very simple and short, because it is difficult for two skippers to skip exactly together at all times. It is also hard to remember your tricks if you try to do too many at once.

Planning a Partner Routine

1. Pick four tricks that both you and your partner know and can do. When you and your partner can do those four tricks together perfectly, then add another four tricks, and so on.

2. Remind each other that each trick should begin with your *right* side (e.g., kick with the right foot or do a Sideswing to the right). You'll both remember the routine more easily, and the tricks will fit together better too.

3. Pick a starting position, such as facing each other or side by side (but remember to do at least eight Two-Foot Bounces to begin so that you are skipping at the same time).

4. Remember to do each trick four times.

Learning and Practising Your Routine

1. After you have decided on the tricks that you'll perform, practise the routine by counting out the "bounces" together, *without using your ropes.* (Give yourself a 1, 2, 3, 4 count introduction so you can begin to bounce together on "1".)

Sample Routine: Suppose that you will do eight Two-Foot Bounces, then four Slaloms, then four Double Unders, then four Crosses, then four Cancans. You would count (out loud): 1, 2, 3, 4 then Two-Foot Bounce on 1, 2, 3, 4, 5, 6, 7, 8, then Slalom (right) on 1, then left for 2, 3, 4, then Double Under on 1, 2, 3, 4, then Two-Foot Bounce on 1, cross arms, bounce on 2, Cross, and continue for 3, 4, then Cancan four times.

Practise your routine until you and your partner can perform the routine *perfectly* without using your ropes.

2. When you can do your routine perfectly without ropes, then, still counting out loud, practise your routine with your partner, using your ropes.

3. When you can perform your partner routine well, go back to the planning stage and add more tricks, or add travelling around while skipping — or skip backwards, and so on.

Note: A really interesting routine usually has some forward and backwards skipping, a turn or two (Half Round, All Round, or Spinner), some kind of Cross and some kind of Double or Triple Under in it.

Using Music

Music adds to your routine and makes it more fun. Pick music that you enjoy, with a good, steady beat. Because you bounce on every beat, be careful that your choice of music is not too fast or too slow.

Two in a Rope

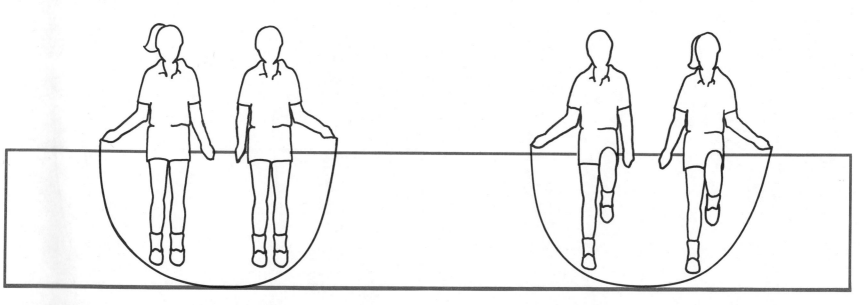

There are different ways that you and a friend can have some fun skipping with one rope. Your rope needs to be a little longer than usual for this.

Each skipper holds a handle (or an end) of the same rope and skips side by side. Both skippers must turn the rope at the same time and jump at the same time. After practising a little, try to make up a routine that you can do together in the rope!

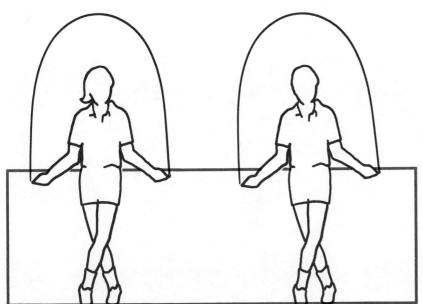
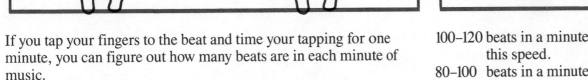
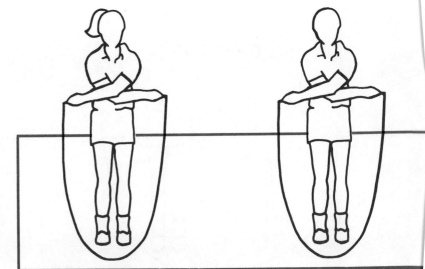

If you tap your fingers to the beat and time your tapping for one minute, you can figure out how many beats are in each minute of music.

140–160 beats in a minute is *very* fast for skipping because you turn your rope on each beat of the music. (If you're in good shape and a good skipper, try it!)

120–140 beats in a minute is a good speed for skipping, especially for doing a routine.

100–120 beats in a minute is rather slow, but you can still skip at this speed.

80–100 beats in a minute is too slow for skipping.

As you get better and better at planning, learning, and performing routines, you may want to try skipping in groups of three, or four, or more!

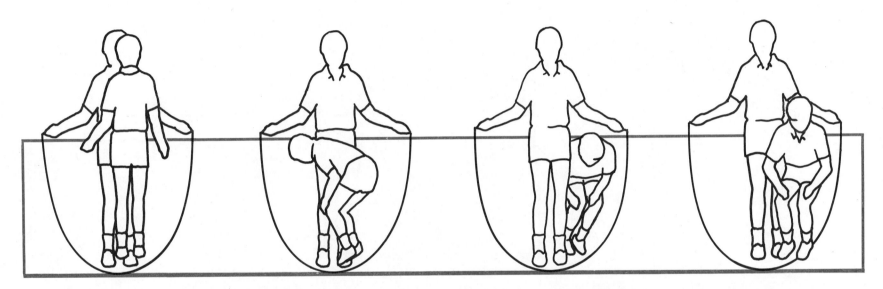

One person can turn the rope for two skippers. A friend jumps at the same time in the rope in front of or behind the rope turner.

Suppose that your friend is turning the rope. Run into your partner's rope from the front just as the rope passes under the turner's feet on its forward turn. You must move in quickly and be close to the turner so that when the rope turns, it will turn around both of you.

Skip slowly, especially at first. When your timing and skipping rhythm improve, you may want to try going around your partner, staying close and jumping when your partner jumps.

It's also possible to do Double Unders with two in a rope!

The Travelling Show

Your rope needs to be a little longer than usual for this trick.

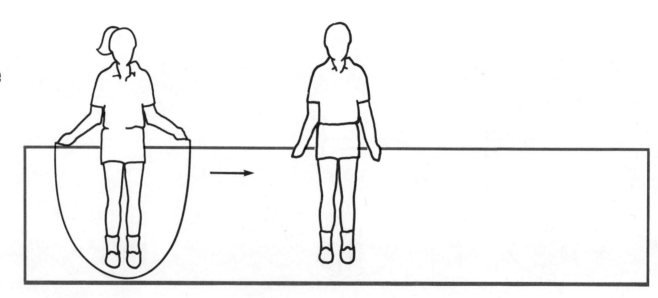

What is the Travelling Show? It's a trick in which one skipper with a rope, called the traveller, moves along a line of jumpers. The traveller skips first with one person in the line, then with a second person in line, then with a third person, and so on.

In this trick, the traveller with the rope moves to each person in the line, rather than the people without the ropes moving to the skipper!

Here's how it works.

You will be the traveller with a skipping rope. Bounce with feet together, moving sideways to the left so that you cover about three-quarters of a metre (two and a half feet) with each Two-Foot Bounce. Practise so that you "travel" to your left on each bounce.

Ask a friend to stand to your left and a little in front of you. Then ask your friend to jump up and down at the same time as you do your bounce.

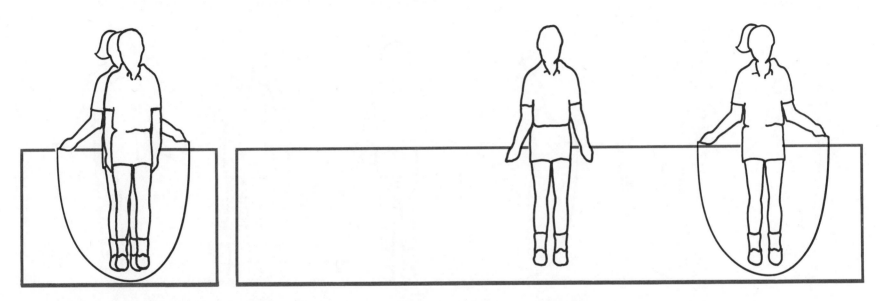

When you both feel you are ready, and your friend is bouncing on the spot at the same speed as you are skipping on the spot, make a sideways Two-Foot Bounce (just as your rope goes behind you), so that you are just behind your friend. Then skip together in the rope for a few bounces.

When you're ready, make another quick sideways jump to your left so that your partner is out of the rope.

As you become more expert at the Travelling Show, do the trick in only three bounces (one alone, one with a partner, and one alone again).

Try the Travelling Show with more friends. You may even want to try jumping in *front* of them, rather than behind.

Double Loops

Practise First

Each rope should be a little longer than usual and this trick works better if the two partners are nearly the same height.

You have to exaggerate your arm actions. That is, turn the ropes using a full turn of your lower arms.

You and your partner must stay *very close* together in the side-by-side position to be able to turn the rope and jump easily.

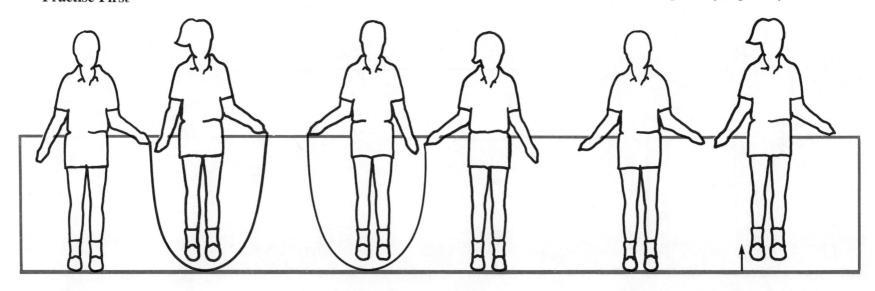

Stand to the right of your partner. First, hold your partner's rope with your inside hand while your partner holds his/her rope with his/her outside hand. Let your partner practise jumping alone at a slow, relaxed speed.

Now hold your own rope with your outside hand while your partner holds your rope with his/her inside hand. You and your partner turn the rope so that you can practise jumping alone.

Now put your ropes down and practise turning and jumping side by side without any ropes. (You'll probably feel a little silly moving your hands and jumping — but it really helps!) Remember that you jump as your outside hand is in the *down* position.

In this trick for two skippers, each skipper holds one handle of his/her own rope in the outside hand and one handle of his/her partner's rope in the inside hand (the hand closest to the partner). When the ropes turn correctly, one skipper jumps one beat ahead of the other.

Turning Two Ropes

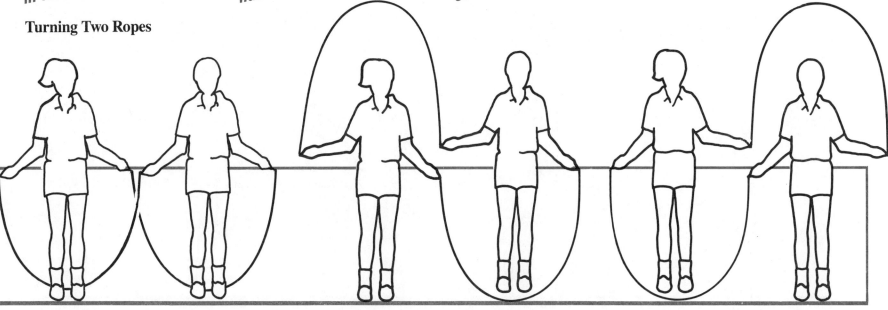

Let your partner's rope be the first one turned. That rope must be *behind* your rope on the ground.

When both you and your partner are ready, call "ready, go" as a signal. On "go," begin to turn your partner's rope in an upward direction. Your partner's outside hand and your inside hand are moving.

Just as the back rope is over your partner's head, begin to turn your own rope. Your outside hand and your partner's inside hand are now moving too. Your partner will jump first, then you will jump just as your partner lands.

Always remember that your outside hand is turning your own rope, so that is what decides when you will jump. You always jump when your outside hand is in the down position. Try not to watch your partner — concentrate on what *you* are doing!

When you and your partner become experts at skipping this way, try a routine. You can even turn all the way around on the spot if you turn *toward* your partner as your inside hand is in the down position (just as your partner is about to jump). To do this, you must keep your hands circling even though you are turning and are not jumping the rope until you complete the turn.

Threes

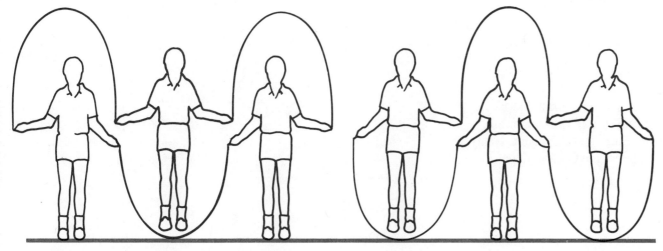

Fours

Wow! What a team effort!

Fives

How many friends can you do this with?

You may want to try this trick with a group of three. Here's how to do it. Line up close together side by side.

The centre skipper jumps when the two outside skippers land, and then the centre skipper lands when the two outside skippers jump.

About the Author

Susan Kalbfleisch has taught health and physical education for sixteen years for the Hamilton (Ontario) Board of Education. She also coaches a demonstration skipping team for the Canadian Heart Foundation and was an executive member of the Ontario Fitness and Health Education Association.